Enjoying
Dog Agility

By Julie Daniels

Second Edition

THE KENNEL CLUB PRO SERIES™
Kennel Club Books® • A Division of BowTie, Inc.

EDITORIAL

Andrew De Prisco	*Editor-in-Chief*
Amy Deputato	*Senior Editor*
Jonathan Nigro	*Associate Editor*
Matt Strubel	*Assistant Editor*

ART

Sherise Buhagiar	*Graphic Design*
Bill Jonas	*Book Design*
Joanne Muzyka	*Digital Graphics*

Kennel Club Books®
A DIVISION OF BOWTIE, INC.
40 Broad Street, Freehold, NJ 07728 • USA

Library of Congress Cataloging-in-Publication Data

Daniels, Julie.
  Enjoying dog agility / by Julie Daniels. — 2nd ed.
     p. cm. — (Kennel Club pro series)
  Includes index.
  ISBN-13: 978-1-59378-661-8
  ISBN-10: 1-59378-661-1
  1. Dogs—Agility trials. 2. Dogs—Training. I. Title.
  SF425.4.D36 2008
  636.7'0888--dc22
                                    2008003345

Printed in China

10   9   8   7   6   5   4   3   2   1

Enjoying
Dog Agility

By Julie Daniels

Second Edition

Acknowledgments

The publisher would like to thank the photographers and owners who contributed photos to this book, including:

Ellen Beris
Scott & Karen Chamberlain
David Dalton
Heather Daniels
Julie Daniels
Joy Elliot
Kendall Fairchild
M. Nicole Fischer Photography
Isabelle Francais
Lisanne Major
SevCo Photography
Sportphotography.ca
Stewart Event Images
Richard Straw
Karen Taylor
United States Dog Agility Association
Gary Wrotnowski
Joyce Yaccarino

Contents

SECTION II: The Obstacles

This book is dedicated to Jessy, the unlikely agility dog who wouldn't settle for less than all-out effort at anything. When Jessy chose agility, our fate was sealed. She chose her friends carefully, stuck with them for life and made them live it to the fullest. I couldn't have asked for more.

Introduction: The FUNdamentals

This book is for helping you learn and enjoy the first-order basics of dog agility training, the FUNdamentals. Agility training begins as simple confidence-building exercises with downscaled obstacles. My way is to separate the elements of difficulty involved on each obstacle and to enjoy each skill conceptually rather than perfunctorily. When the skills are put together this way, the dog doesn't just tolerate the obstacle, he loves it and feels great pride in performing it. This is a wonderful start to a long and successful competition career, to be sure, but that enjoyment and pride also transfer readily to the dog's everyday life even if competition is not for you. At any level, this sport invites you to develop a closer bond with your dog than you may ever have imagined.

Like many sports, dog agility is open to anyone who wants to participate. From the moment you decide that you would enjoy running around a large obstacle course to direct your dog over, under, around and through various challenges that you have learned together, think of agility as a team sport. This book is for helping you learn the joys and requirements of the sport and for helping you nurture that same combination of fun, athletics and teamwork in your canine partner.

SECTION I

THIS
IS
AGILITY

CHAPTER 1

A Contest of Fun

Welcome to an exciting young sport begun in England as an extra mode of entertainment to fill time between events at the world-famous Crufts International Dog Show in 1978. Named dog agility, the event was such a hit with the spectators and the participants that a new dog sport was born.

With agility there's a whole new possibility for fun and teamwork with your dog. A fine agility course is an impressive and irresistible sight; it looks like a super-playground for dogs. The colors are vivid, bright and

> *Money will buy a pretty good dog, but it won't buy the wag of his tail.*
> —Josh Billings

shining; the hefty equipment just calls out for playtime, and there's plenty of room for you and all your friends. The fast-paced action of agility seems to draw spectators from out of the woodwork. Audiences seem to run the course vicariously as the dogs tear around the field, working the course with tails wagging and muscles rippling. The handlers have the job of directing their dogs and helping them do well, but it is certainly the dogs that are in the limelight during competition.

Dog agility thrived as a sport in England due to the hard work and dedication of several key players and training organizations. Needless to say, many people contributed a great deal of time and effort to building equipment, instructing newcomers and bringing the sport to new locations. For every person who appears in the spotlight, dozens more have worked hard behind the scenes. Thanks must be given to all these people and to their unified goal of developing agility as an athletic sport with the emphasis on fun. Due to their efforts, agility now has such a large following around the world that it draws capacity crowds of competitors and spectators.

Over the last few decades, many variations of the sport have sprung up; some of them, in Europe and in the US, are quite far removed from agility's original intent and guidelines. Like any new sport, agility is vulnerable to different interpretations from different people; fortunately, international standards are now being adopted. This is the sensible thing to do, as it will ensure that the sport enjoys recognized international terminology and a consensus of inter-pretation as worldwide competitions become more popular.

AGILITY IN THE US: A VERY BRIEF HISTORY

The United States Dog Agility Association (USDAA) was established in 1985 and incorporated in 1986 as a sole proprietorship to promote English-style dog agility in this country. Coincidentally, the first two enthusiasts to build English-style agility equipment and begin organizing its introduction were both from the state of Texas, though they did not know of each other. Sandra Davis from El Paso and Kenneth Tatsch

This fun-loving group attended an agility camp at the author's White Mountain Agility facility.

from Dallas began using their knowledge of the sport in England to build proper equipment in the US. Each continued communicating with experts overseas in order to remain true to the sport as it was intended, and it was through that avenue that they were made aware of each other.

In a country as large as the United States, nothing short of a major campaign would be enough to promote a new sport at the national level. Without central guidance and regular communication with agility authorities in England, there would be no hope of maintaining the integrity and focus of the sport as word and interest spread. With the help of underwriting from Pedigree dog foods (also called Kal Kan in the US), Kenneth Tatsch set about organizing a national tournament that would attract the best agility competitors from all parts of the country.

This event, known as the Pedigree Grand Prix of Dog Agility, made its debut in 1988 in conjunction with the prestigious Astro World Series of Dog Shows held at the Astrodome complex in Houston, Texas. The intent was to promote agility in all corners of the country. Because travel across the US can be prohibitively expensive, it was the practice from the beginning for Pedigree to pay the expenses of regional winners to allow them to travel to Houston for the national semifinals and finals.

The Grand Prix tournament has been highly successful and has made many friends for agility. In 1990, the number of regional qualifying trials was increased to 16 (up from 10 in 1989) to accommodate the sport's increased popularity while keeping the rapid growth under control. Perhaps the growth of the sport in the United States is best measured by spectator interest at the nationals. There was some interest in agility in 1988, although most spectators did not know what they were watching. In 1989, nearly 2,000 people attended the Grand Prix's finals competition, which was taped for national TV. In 1990, not only did agility have extensive TV coverage but it also had an overwhelming command of the crowds. Stands on both sides of the agility arena were packed with an estimated 4,000 cheering fans.

In 1989, again following the English lead, it was decided to introduce dog agility at a major US horse show. Kenneth Tatsch, again sponsored by Pedigree, called upon five of the Northeast's top agility dogs. These were Bach (Brenda Bruja), Brownie (Jean MacKenzie), Val (Ron and Cheryl Pitkin) and my dog Jessy, all prizewinners from the New England Agility Team; the fifth was Cooper (Alaina Axford), a national finalist from Pennsylvania. The handlers volunteered days of preparation, travel and work to put on demonstrations and offer one-on-one introductory instruction for many new enthusiasts at the Radnor Hunt International Horse Show in Pennsylvania.

As a result, Brenda, Cheryl, Ron and I combined forces to transport a complete regulation agility course 400 miles to the show site. We also brought a great deal of downscaled equipment for training newcomers. Jean joined us in New York, and Alaina met us at the show site along with Kenneth. There we all worked for four long wonderful days in the rain, sun, wind and chill that Pennsylvania enjoys in October. The overwhelming success of that week's work put agility on the program at several of the US's top horse shows in 1990. A forum such as a horse show, so spacious and athletic, seems quite well suited to this sport.

In May of 1990, the very first agility titling event was held under the auspices of the USDAA. At the BB Agility Center in Danville, Virginia, dogs and handlers from all over the country gathered to try the first sanctioned test. Our judge was Sue Henry from Texas, and she set up some challenges that had us very worried, though they would be considered basic by today's standards. On that day, the first dog to get around the course without faults was Alaina

In the early days, agility enthusiasts literally brought the sport to new locations.

A scene from a regional championship. A "shanty town" pops up around the course as exhibitors set up tents to keep themselves and their dogs in the shade and to protect their gear.

Axford's Portuguese Water Dog Cooper. In all, six dogs earned the Agility Dog title offered by the USDAA. Blue handwritten certificates were fashioned on the spot for the six qualifying dogs. I still have both of mine, and they are among my most precious agility keepsakes! The five successful handlers included Alaina with Cooper, Marilyn Belli with Vizsla Jessie, Sally Glei with Border Collie Sophie, Fran Hoffman with Manchester Terrier Ali and me with Rottweiler Jessy and English Springer Spaniel Arrow.

Agility was originally developed by combining the challenges of stadium jumping in the horse world with different challenges unique to dogs. These included many from the canine obstacle courses used by the military. Some, such as the wall, were modified for agility in the interests of safety and smaller dogs.

Other obstacles were made more difficult, and additional ones were added to emphasize specific skills such as balancing, flexing, tunneling and jumping. Agility courses are designed to test a dog's fitness, flexibility and responsiveness. Obviously the jumps inspired by the horse world had to be adapted for dogs. Nevertheless, the two natural parents of dog agility, stadium jumping and military K-9 courses, can both be seen clearly in the sport today.

The American Kennel Club (AKC) organized its first agility titling program and sponsored a wonderful first trial in Houston, Texas in 1995. The AKC's program differs markedly from the USDAA's version and is widely considered more doable for a wider variety of dogs. There are a few other sanctioning organizations in the US as well, and we are lucky to have them all. It's terrific that we have in this country more than one venue in which to enjoy various interpretations of dog agility. The only downside to the AKC's program is that it is currently open only to purebred dogs recognized by the American Kennel Club. This represents just a fraction of the dog population in this country, and an even smaller fraction of the purebred dog population recognized elsewhere in the world by international agility organizations. Perhaps this restriction will be changed in the interest of allowing more dogs to take part in the AKC's wonderful agility program. The other US organizations welcome all dogs, mixed breed and purebred, registered and unregistered, as do some of the international tournaments.

AGILITY OBSTACLES AND COURSES

Dog agility combines a fast pace, physical challenges, strategy and teamwork. And let's not forget sheer enjoyment. Everywhere the sport is intro- duced, dogs, handlers, volunteers and spectators alike are falling in love with the crazy, fun-filled games that help give agility its name.

This sport invites each dog/handler team to negotiate an obstacle course. The handler serves as

Flexibility, precision and lightning speed are three key elements in conquering the weave poles.

team captain, navigator and chief strategist. The dog does the hard part: following his handler's directions and negotiating the obstacles. Each course challenges the team to get from start to finish through an array of open and closed tunnels, weave poles, dogwalks, seesaws, A-frames, pause tables, tire jumps and many other types of jumps. For clarification, we can group the obstacles by the type of challenge they represent.

The first group of obstacles contains those that require the dog to put his whole body through something. These apertures include open and closed tunnels and tire jumps. The open tunnel consists of a long tube; in competition, the tube is often bent to create sharp turns. The closed tunnel begins with a rigid opening, but the dog must then push his way through a long collapsed chute made of canvas or nylon. The tire is a hoop or ring raised up in a strong framework; the dog must jump through its large opening.

The next group of obstacles requires the dog to climb. These are the ramps, including the A-frame, dogwalk and seesaw. The A-frame is composed of two 9-foot ramps, leaned and secured against each other. The dog must go up one side, over the top and all the way down the other side.

The dogwalk consists of narrow planks, each about 12 feet long, going up, across and down. Technically it is a catwalk, but, as that name was incongruous with this sport, the English originators of agility settled on the nickname dogwalk. The highest point of an agility dogwalk is between 4 and 4-$\frac{1}{2}$ feet off the ground.

The seesaw is just that, a teeter-totter, and the dog must walk up far enough to tip the raised end down and continue down the plank to dismount.

Each of these ramp obstacles is designed to have us teach the dog to ascend and descend safely. This is measured by whether the dog touches the specially painted contact zones on the end of each ramp. Contact zones are painted in a contrasting color to the rest of the ramp. In the US the zones are yellow, but that is not the prevalent color overseas.

The next group of obstacles is the jumps. Jumps are a major part of an agility course and they come in all kinds. There are hurdles (some with decorative supports called "wings" on each side), single and double bar jumps, panels, spread jumps (both deep and high), broad jumps that are low and very deep and others. The height of the jumps for a given dog is determined by the height classification of the dog as measured to the top of his shoulder blades.

Another type of obstacle is the pause table, which tests the dog's willingness to interrupt his run and stay in a designated spot in a certain position until the handler directs otherwise. The table is a raised

The fast-paced energy and the dogs' enthusiasm garnered many spectators and participants for the sport of agility.

platform that measures 3 feet square. The dog must get onto the table and stay in the required position for a count of five seconds. The judge (or electronic timer) counts backwards from five to one, then says "Go," at which point the dog may leave. It's the epitome of "hurry up and wait."

The weave poles are probably the most impressive obstacle in agility. The dog must travel just so down a single row of vertical poles, flexing left and right to go around them, slalom style. The row consists of 6 to 12 poles, generally made of PVC pipe. Poles are usually about 21 inches apart. The dog must enter the line of poles from right to left and may not miss a single one. The speed at which some dogs can accomplish this feat, sometimes pushing three poles at once in different directions, leaves spectators shaking their heads. Our fastest dogs can weave 12 poles in 2 seconds.

In agility competitions, also called agility trials, courses are not generally duplicated, so sequences cannot be trained by rote. Participants do not know until shortly before start time just what obstacle layout and sequence will be assigned. A standard time for the course is set according to the length and difficulty of that particular course. Standard course time describes the number of seconds deemed to be the maximum amount of time a team should take to complete the course without penalty. Different levels of difficulty entail different numbers of obstacles, but a top-level course is usually composed of 20 obstacle challenges.

Each dog/handler team is judged and timed individually. Course faults are assessed for incorrect performance on any obstacle. Time faults accrue against each team that takes longer than the standard course time to complete the run. Depending on time and other constraints of the day's schedule, the judge often sets a maximum course time (MCT), after which a dog/handler team will be eliminated. Other causes for elimination may include aggressive behavior, soiling the course, poor sportsmanship, leaving the course area and excessive assistance from the handler or from outside the ring. In some classes, elimination also results from other factors like accruing three refusals during a course run, taking the wrong course route, skipping an obstacle or exceeding the maximum fault limit.

Particulars of the course and the judge's intended scoring of the class are explained to the assembled competitors during the judge's briefing, after the course has been set up for the running of the class. An informal map of the course layout is generally posted, and copies might be made available for exhibitors, although this is not required. A numbered marker is placed at each obstacle to help everyone learn the required order in which the course is to be run. We've mentioned that no two courses are exactly alike, so the dogs cannot memorize their assignments. The handlers must therefore be the navigators.

Immediately before or after the judge's briefing, handlers get the chance to walk the course without their dogs in order to plan the strategy of their individual runs. Then the test begins, with each dog/handler team taking a turn at the course, one height division at a time.

In a sanctioned test, the handler may not touch the dog or the obstacles without incurring faults, but the handler is free to signal and talk to his dog nonstop, calling out commands and encouraging all he wants. The crowd often plays an important, noisy role in keeping the excitement level high.

Some competitions call for each dog/handler team to compete in two rounds over two different courses, with either the better score or (usually) the cumulative score being taken. Other contests, often when the field is down to the finalists in the event, are a one-shot run. A perfect score is called "clean" or "clear." All else being equal, the fastest time wins. However, trying to work the course as fast as possible often causes the dogs to make mistakes, such as missing a contact zone or knocking off a jump bar. Each is penalized. Speed is commonly a tiebreaker among clear rounds, and course times are taken, usually by an electronic timer rather than a hand-held stop watch, to the hundredth of a second.

Most countries have in place a system for offering agility titles to competitors who meet certain

Whether your dog is large and big-boned, lean and lithe or long and low, there is a place in agility for him.

standards. But agility tests are a lot more than titles. Competitions might feature various games classes in addition to the standard agility and jumping classes. Most participants enter more than one class at a day's event. There are special classes that are less demanding for new or veteran dogs and a rapidly expanding Junior Handler program, which is so important to the future vitality of the sport. More new game classes are always appearing, which are often quite imaginative and always great fun.

EVERY DOG CAN BENEFIT

Keeping in mind that this sport has a lot to offer anyone, whether competition is of interest or not, it's fun to speculate about just what makes a good agility partnership between a handler and his dog.

There are many people today, both children and adults, who have close active relationships with their dogs. The relationships between these people and their pets have many of the mental and physical characteristics of a first-rate agility team. Whether they ever join dog agility classes or enter competitions, agility is part of their way of life. And a rich life it is, whether their dogs are purebred or mixed, large or small. The sport of agility offers many new twists, even if you think there's nothing you and your dog don't already know about camaraderie.

I see many dogs that desperately need a place to put their energies and many owners, young and not-so-young, who would like to be able to enjoy a better life with their dogs. Agility is a positive thing to do, a step in the right direction. It just might give you the extra motivation it takes to tackle your mutual problems, so you and your dog can learn to understand and appreciate each other.

As for the physical characteristics of a natural agility dog, it is usually assumed that a relatively lightweight, lithe body type is the choice for agility. As different jump heights for shorter dogs are adopted, the height of the dog becomes less important, but different agility flavors (venues) define their height divisions differently, so obtain a copy of the agility regulations that affect your dog. Because the sport is still young, there will be many changes still to come, involving jump heights, obstacles, rules and judging parameters. The only way to keep abreast of the changes that affect you is to join your national agility organization and read the newsletters.

How much does your dog weigh? How tall is he at the withers (shoulders)? An easy way to determine this height is to stand a yardstick next to his front leg and lay a level across the top of his withers. My own experience is that a weight to height ratio of less than 2-$\frac{1}{2}$ pounds to 1 pound per inch is good for agility. Of course, other factors can tip the scale in favor of enjoying competition with a dog who doesn't fit the ideal picture. Many dogs who are big, short or heavy have provided some surprises for the agility world.

If you are out to choose a dog for agility, one who has the right stuff going in, look for a nimble

National Agility Organizations in the US

Agility is exploding in popularity in the United States. We are fortunate, in our large country, to have a variety of agility venues to choose from. It's fair to say that there is an agility competition and title available for any sound and healthy dog, from the highest international standard to the most elementary basic skills. Following is only a partial list; while these organizations account for most of the competitions available throughout the United States, they are by no means the only venues. Two good websites to visit for a list of activities sponsored by many different agility organizations are **www.agilityevents.net** and **www.cleanrun.com**.

- American Kennel Club **www.akc.org**
- Canine Performance Events **www.k9cpe.com**
- North American Dog Agility Council **www.nadac.com**
- United Kennel Club **www.unitedkennelclub.com**
- United States Dog Agility Association **www.usdaa.com**

dog. Choose one who is sound, curious and confident and who likes people. If you're looking at puppies, think in terms of his maturing at a height and size that will be comfortable for competition. Right away, join your national agility organization in order to keep up with this fast-growing sport. You may also find a local club or class that you would enjoy and that would provide opportunities for regular work on regulation equipment and news of local agility events.

National Agility Organizations in Canada

The Canadian agility programs were influenced by the early start-ups in the United States, but Canada's programs have remained distinct and have evolved to have important differences from those in the United States. Many competitors from both countries enjoy competing across the border.

- Agility Association of Canada **www.aac.ca**
- Canadian Kennel Club **www.ckc.ca**

Regulations will dictate whether you may compete with smaller dogs at lowered jump heights; this makes a great difference in the dogs many people will choose for agility competition. If you already have a dog that is healthy, is active, likes to jump and can be taught to take direction from you, don't rule out agility. It combines athletics with lots of casual fun.

Competition aside, agility training can benefit all dogs, but you need to make use of what is good for your dog and avoid putting him to challenges that are unsuitable for him. There are some very large dogs that live very active lives and have bodies that can withstand rigorous agility work. A giant dog who is very fit may do well, and the two of you can have a lot of fun. However, extremely big dogs are not candidates for agility competition at the highest international jump height of 26 inches. That said, the most important benefit of agility training for dogs is in helping them use and enjoy their bodies and minds more fully.

I had a large male Rottweiler that was trim, strong and confident at two years old. He was in terrific shape and always enjoyed agility. His weight to height ratio was more than four to one, well into the danger zone. As with all big dogs, his body was slow to mature, still broadening with age, so all his early jump training was done at low heights. He sailed over full-height jumps on his own given the chance and, like many other agility dogs, he could put his coordination to his own use now and then. While waiting his turn in the back of my parked pickup at the agility field, he would sometimes hop out between the closed tailgate and the raised hatch of the truck cap.

Once, when I saw him do this, I yelled at him, and he spun around and easily hopped from the ground over the raised tailgate to get back in. It seems that with a dog that was so agile I might as well have gone all out, but I believe it would have taken a nasty toll on his body over a few years. The agility title classes are difficult by any standards and especially rigorous for a big dog. It was a difficult decision since he loved the sport. Ultimately I titled him (back then, that meant jumping 30 inches) at age 3.

Does your own dog have any physical characteristic that should make you think twice about competing in agility with him? A dog that has a long back and short legs is at risk of back injury. Any dog that has chronic soreness is at risk, and don't think that giving pain killers protects your dog from injury—quite the opposite. A dog that is out of shape is at increased risk from all sorts of injury. Weigh the risks and benefits and consider them carefully. Any dog should be sound and healthy before beginning a training program.

Agility is a sport that gives as good as it gets. You don't need to have your eye on competition, or even a complete agility course, in order to enjoy basic agility training, and all dogs can gain something in the process. For example, a high level of confidence is a plus in agility, but agility training itself can be a wonderful confidence builder for timid dogs. Further, your dog needs to be controllable to compete in agility, but basic agility training can help you establish that control in a positive way. An agility competitor must be strong, brisk and flexible, but any dog can learn some introductory agility exercises and come out stronger, faster and more supple than he started.

How about your dog or a dog you know? Dog agility is a wonderful activity for purebred dogs and mixed breeds, young people and adults, beginners and more experienced participants. If you and your dog would like a little more exercise, a little more fun and a bit of a challenge, then try this terrific sport and see where it leads you.

CHAPTER 2

Getting Started

"A" IS FOR ATTITUDE

There is nothing more important to education than a positive attitude. Your dog's attitude toward new things has been shaped to some extent up to this point. He may approach physical challenges with delight, he may brave some novelties and fear others or he may view anything new with misgivings.

> *If a man neglects education, he walks lame to the end of his life.*
> —Plato

In any case, you can do wonderful things for your dog by introducing agility training. Agility can help shy dogs feel proud and give active dogs a welcome outlet for their energies. It can boost self-confidence in the insecure dog and sprinkle confidence with common sense in the independent dog. What it can do for you and your dog together depends mostly on you.

Your dog's attitude is the first thing to consider each time you pick up his leash. What are your goals in this sport? What are you trying to accomplish with your dog today? How can you break that goal down into manageable steps and sensible progressions so that you and your dog will become a better team for the day's lessons?

If you don't feel relaxed about a certain lesson, neither will your student, the dog. Instead of going ahead with a lesson that you don't feel comfortable with, you should either review a previous lesson that was enjoyable to your dog and at which he was successful or introduce an easier version of the lesson you had planned. You can also skip the lesson and go back to it another time. Whatever you do, don't let an introduction to a new lesson go badly.

Here are three basic guidelines for developing the positive attitude you and your dog need in order to get the most from your mutual education and from agility in particular:

1. Attitude comes first, before the task is mastered. Like it or not, you are shaping attitude with guidance, with corrections and rewards and with the feeling you project.
2. Begin your dog's training with exercises that are easier than you think he needs and progress only when your dog needs more challenge, not when you do. A positive attitude toward the first agility obstacles comes from quick early success. When you hit a real snag later on, leave that lesson alone for a week or so while you go back to those delightful basics.
3. Don't let someone else's timetable for progress dictate your own. Each dog has a distinctive way of learning and needs help from his handler differently. Choose your training times, enticements and challenges according to what will best strengthen your dog's educational foundation.

Keeping all these things in mind, it is important to think positively. It will make you a better handler and your dog a better partner. Be certain to take your time. Humans are always in such a hurry. A big problem with rushing training, particularly in an active sport like agility, is that it puts on pressure too soon, which undermines the happiness your dog feels for achieving the basics.

Without a positive attitude toward the introductory levels of training, your dog has limited happiness to fall back on when you have training problems later and need to review the basics, as we all do. When you rush through the first steps, or skip them and get right to the hard part, you are building a weak foundation. Even if you have a brave, outgoing dog that seems able to handle it at the time, sooner or later you will be teaching your dog to fail.

Instead, introduce your dog to obedience and agility tasks that he can master quickly and enjoy these first successes thoroughly. You will see a wide variety of dogs' innate abilities displayed in agility. Some dogs need more time at the introductory levels on tunnel obstacles, while other dogs can progress quickly on the tunnels and need more time with the inclines. The important thing is to ensure early success, which builds a strong and willing spirit. Your dog will learn to succeed, like to succeed and expect to succeed.

By the time you have taught your first dog his first agility obstacle, you and your dog will share a similar attitude. Are we having fun yet?

CLICKER TRAINING

The sport of dog agility calls for a dog and handler who can work independently yet together at the same time and have fun doing it. If you can't yet control your dog in a positive way, there are many classes and books that can help you.

A clicker shaping session on a downscaled ramp; notice the green clicker in the handler's left hand. You can start even a young puppy with this type of training.

My personal recommendation is clicker training. Clicker training is the epitome of "catching them doing something right." It's a wonderful way to help your dog recognize the behaviors that we want to develop in an agility dog. Our family pets regularly exhibit behaviors that affect their environment and get our attention. Why not mark (with a click) those behaviors that we want him to use and follow through with a reward so he connects the positive consequences with the behaviors that earn a click? The reward is the crux of clicker training and why it works so well. It is a "win-win" approach to dog training. If we show the dog which behaviors will allow him to get what he wants, he will return to these behaviors by choice in the future. We all use what works. Check out the clicker-training website www.clickertraining.com for a wealth of information and many good books to consider.

Clicker training is all the rage nowadays, and not all of it is well done. Pay attention to the details. Keep your clicking "clean." Capture a piece of behavior with your click and then quickly move the treat to the dog. That is the proper order of events. By the way, if your own reflexes are slow, work on that separately. Playing the two-person hand game slapjack sharpens your manual quickness.

You may also want to find a good basic obedience class, again choosing one that uses the clicker method. A good class has happy dogs with wagging tails and smiling owners! The clicker approach is perfect for agility, because in our sport the dog has

Using clicker training to teach tricks is a great way to sharpen your clicker skills, which will improve your agility handling. This English Springer demonstrates a "wave."

to make many performance decisions. When he hears you click, he knows that at that moment he has made a good decision and has earned a treat. Of course, a "treat" can be anything that your dog will work for; you are not limited to food or toys. Food and toys are the most common choices for treats, but depending on the dog and the circumstances, something like going outside or greeting a friend can be a motivating treat. The dog's mindset determines what is of value to him at any given moment, so a "treat" simply means something he's willing to work for right now.

Of course some control is necessary for agility training. On the other hand, if you are used to exercising an extreme amount of control over your dog, you may need to loosen up a little in order to help him think for himself, which he will have to do in order to perform in agility. This sport is not for a robot. The dog is a thinking partner in negotiating all of the obstacles and pathways on an agility course. The best teachers are mindful that good training is a two-way feedback system.

FUN AND GAMES

With good training in mind, there are many things you can do around the house with your dog to further your agility teamwork. Whatever your home environment, you can find fun and games that will help you and your dog understand and enjoy each other. First, you must make the commitment to work and play with your dog. The best agility-minded games for you to play with your dog every day are those that enhance your relationship, emphasizing both athleticism and fun. Here are brief descriptions of a few of my favorites.

JUMPING INTO YOUR ARMS

This activity improves coordination and timing for both of you and jumping confidence for your dog.

Teach him by sitting in a chair, patting your leg and getting him to put his front paws on your leg by invitation so you can scoop him up. As he gets more eager, encourage him to jump into your lap. Once he enjoys this game, play it without the chair. Bend your knees at first and gradually stand more and more erect. This method teaches your dog to jump across your body rather than directly at your front. Don't teach a big dog to jump straight onto your chest unless you want him jumping into your face!

PLAYING CATCH

Teach your dog to catch on leash at first, and make sure you can get the toy back to try again. No corrections. No reprimands. Just keep tossing the object gently and go crazy with delight when he succeeds. I have taught this game even to dogs who seemed hopelessly uncoordinated with it at first. It improves their reflexes and agility and it helps them learn to watch you and concentrate. The talented ones can learn to catch from quite a distance. Make sure you use something that cannot get lodged in your dog's throat if he catches it too aggressively. A small stuffed toy is great and is easier for the novice dog to nab than the ever-popular tennis ball. Don't take it away from him right away! Let him strut on leash while you clap and cheer.

For early catch training, especially if your dog likes food better than toys, my favorite choice is popcorn. It is easy to toss and easy for the dog to catch. Remember to keep a cheerful demeanor and a positive attitude. It's the most delightful feeling when your hardworking student finally grabs the goodie in midair and you both become ecstatic over it. You can play tug with him if he likes that. As for popcorn, my way is to give the dog a quick piece for free every time he catches one in the air.

A simple game of catch can build important skills that you will use in agility training.

You could cheerfully scoop up the ones that hit the floor, but if you give a free piece for each catch, the dog will learn to catch even if you let him eat the pieces off the floor.

Backing Up

Teaching a dog to back up improves any dog's coordination and body awareness and teaches him to shift his center of gravity back, which will be very useful when he has to find a difficult weave pole entry, hit his contact zones in the rain or collect his stride for a tight jump sequence. You will get a lot of use out of this simple parlor trick!

To teach this, I just use a cookie or toy and put it between the dog's front legs. As he bends his head to follow it, I click and then give it to him. That's step one. After just a couple of repetitions of that simple move to get his head down, I can move the toy backward under the dog's belly and click when he shifts his weight back. After a couple of repetitions of that maneuver, I can delay the click until he actually moves one of his feet backward (then two feet, and so on). This process of building a complex behavior in simple progressive steps is called "shaping" the behavior. The clicker is a powerful training tool for marking the increments of progress along the way. Practice your timing and pay attention to the piece of behavior you are trying to capture with the click.

UNEXPECTED SUBSTRATES

The best way to prepare for unexpected quirks on an agility course later is to get used to as many unusual situations as possible from this moment on. It's important to introduce these challenges to your dog in a constructive way. If you let him feel insecure upon the first introduction, then you make it much harder to build his confidence. When introducing strange substrates, begin with situations that are different but not frightening for your dog. Is your dog willing to walk over unusual surfaces, like rustling plastic or slippery linoleum? Get out the treats or his favorite toy and make sure he associates the new surface with something pleasant. Your clicker can help you. Use the same approach on the next new encounter, such as a plank you've set up securely on cinder blocks.

REWARDING YOUR DOG

I recommend using toys or morsels of food when introducing something new to prevent the new encounter from causing the dog stress. Any training tool can be abused, food included. Make sure you are paying for his efforts, not for failure! Break the job down into easy pieces so you can ensure success. This is true for both the games you play in training and for the regulation agility obstacles. Click early and often!

Don't worry that you will not be able to wean your dog from the rewards once it's time for him to run an agility course, where you are not allowed to carry them. You will certainly be able to teach your dog to run an agility course without stuffing him with treats throughout. But that is down the road and this is now. You will also teach your dog to run the course without his collar and leash, but that does not mean that the collar and leash are not good tools for early learning. As with food and any other enticements, gradually use them less blatantly and then less often as the individual task becomes familiar and fun for the dog.

Your first job is to make sure that your dog has pleasant experiences when introduced to each obstacle. Some dogs seem to be more careful on the equipment if no distraction is offered until the obstacle is completed, but remember that accuracy is not the dog's first job. It's the handler's job to keep the enticement in the right place to keep the dog where he's supposed to be. You may want to use a strong enticement at first, even when it makes your dog super eager, because it also ensures that he is delighted to be on the equipment.

Once your dog is more familiar with an obstacle, offer enticements less often until the next new task. Use your own judgment, but don't get locked into a mindset that won't let you see when the dog's confidence would be enhanced by goodies. Your dog will learn to handle the stress and the details of the sport as he gets used to it, provided that he enjoys himself early on. Keep an open mind. Don't categorically

Reward your dog with anything that he enjoys.

dismiss props such as a clicker, food, toys, a leash, a collar, tummy-rubbing, play training or silly antics from your cache of training tools. You just might need them all, and they just might make it more fun.

It is quite possible to instruct your dog on the various regulation agility obstacles without giving him a sense of fun about it all. What a shame that would be! If you incorporate obstacles of all kinds into the fun you have with your dog every day, and incidentally introduce specific agility equipment as part of an interesting day, then you are appreciating the sport. It becomes part of the quality time you spend with your dog. Whether or not you have any interest in competing in agility trials, the sport offers you and your dog another dimension in good clean fun.

IMPROVE YOUR DOG'S IQ

When you add a dog to your family, the quality of that pet's life depends on you. To help your dog reach his full potential, you need to be caregiver, companion, teacher and friend. If you want a smart dog, keep his life happy and stimulating. If you want a smart dog who is a pleasure to live with, you must also educate him. It's not your dog's job to be human, but if you will accept the responsibility of teaching him the rules and manners of his human family, you can enrich your family life a great deal. There's no substitute for the work this entails, but the rewards last forever.

Agility training is one of the most effective ways of teaching your dog to use his brain constructively, as it puts obedience to work in a whole new way. It's so much fun that you and your dog will love to practice, and practicing the fundamentals of agility improves basic obedience at the same time.

The basic obedience commands (sit, down, stay, come and heel) are not just challenges for the dog, they are mind/body challenges for each dog/handler team. For many years, I've used agility obstacles to

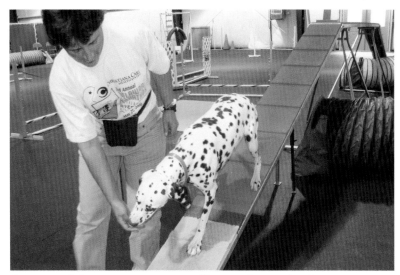

As your training progresses, you will reward your dog for very specific behaviors; in this case, for touching the yellow contact zone at the bottom of the ramp.

help get this perspective across in all of my obedience classes. Agility work helps us look at obedience lessons as combined physical and mental efforts, and it accelerates the building of trust, confidence and teamwork into our human/canine partnerships. In my opinion, it also makes a dog smarter, because he learns a lot about problem solving, taking unexpected challenges in stride, working with his handler and coordinating his body with his mind. It is also bound to improve some of these abilities in you, too, so you can expect to become a smarter dog handler.

In learning to encourage and reward your dog, you will begin to develop a stronger rapport with your pet and you will begin to see challenges from the dog's point of view. For example, when you introduce a tunnel, and you know that it's your job to inspire your dog to go through it, you begin to appreciate the dog's work as well as your own. You must also rise to the task of motivating your dog.

And who among us, human or canine, is not interested in a new twist now and then? That's what keeps our brains in gear. If we don't give ourselves something creative to do now and then, it is only a matter of time before boredom gets the better of us.

No doubt about it, if your dog's environment is boring, and your dog is a bright dog, sooner or later he will discover a pastime that is interesting to him but unacceptable to you. The first thing you must promise yourself in agility training could be that you will take the time to vary your dog's environment in a positive way. That doesn't mean locking him in the garage instead of the cellar every other day. It really requires you to introduce him to novel stimuli every day with you on the other end of the leash. Remember, what is novel to one dog could be old hat to another, so choose the stimuli you introduce with your own dog's personality and experience in mind.

The perfect new encounter is something that challenges your dog to accept something different, but not so different that he cannot succeed readily. If your dog is extremely active and outgoing, you might begin by having him walk politely on leash. If your dog is terribly shy, you might have him join you in watching children play from an appropriate distance. In both cases, the best initial distance between you and distraction depends upon your dog and you.

You can work up to more interesting challenges by building a firm base of incremental successes. It's most important that each new introduction goes smoothly, so your dog can steadily gain experience and confidence without being a nuisance.

Agility training can be part of this gradual widening of your dog's world. My favorite agility obstacles to begin with are various tunnels and A-frames. In this book you will be introduced to several versions of these obstacles, which you can easily fashion at home to start improving your dog's IQ.

At the same time, you'll be improving his agility quotient (AQ, of course).

You probably know at least a couple of bright dogs who are wasting their brains and engaging in activities that you aren't fond of. These undesirable behaviors could probably be channeled into happy, positive pursuits. Many of the best-known canine movie stars, police drug-search dogs, hearing ear dogs, etc., were rescued from animal shelters where they would otherwise have been just another statistic in the ever-growing problem of owner unpreparedness and lack of commitment. It warms my heart to know that some dogs graduate from backyards or animal shelters and are given an education, which some of us take so much for granted. It hurts to know that millions more dogs never find a fulfilling life, yet some people keep breeding puppies and more puppies, never accepting responsibility for the quality of their lives.

Perhaps more people nowadays feel unsatisfied, and that makes them less sensitive to the needs of animals. But if you tune in to your own dog and bring fulfillment to his life, he will invariably do the same for you. It's good to understand your dog's outlook, so basic and honest and different from your own. What a bonus that your dog readily accepts your looks and quirks and imperfections.

For many of us, dogs are members of the family. We raise them, educate them, work and play with them and enjoy a family life all the richer for their being with us. We have the privileges and opportunities to broaden our lives when we live with dogs.

Is your dog healthy, strong and clean? He deserves to be. Does he enjoy doing things with you? Why not start his education today? Get help from a dog obedience trainer who has a philosophy compatible with your own. Look through the many quality books available, again choosing what is comfortable for you and what will help you meet your goals. Dogs are wonderful and complicated companions. The sport of agility is just one more way for us to work and play with them. You may decide as you and your dog improve that you are interested in agility competition. You don't have to compete in order to enjoy the sport. Its greatest value is in strengthening the bond between you and your dog and giving the both of you something new, active, challenging and fun to do together.

FUNDAMENTALS—OBEDIENCE FOR AGILITY

Whether you enroll in a class or learn from training books, you will want to give your dog a good foundation in manners and the basic obedience commands. In agility you will need directives for having your dog come to you, lie down, sit, stay and run with you. These cues need to be understood and accepted by your dog so well that he will obey them even in the excitement of running an agility course. For everyday living, these social skills are required of a well-mannered pet who will be welcome wherever his owner goes. In regard to obedience training, as with obstacle training, the dog's acceptance of these commands, along with his attitude toward them, is largely the owner's responsibility.

For agility training, your dog should learn to sit and lie down instantly on command and stay until called, even in the midst of a rousing run through the obstacles. He must come to you when called, especially when he is running the opposite way, and it's an advantage for him to know how to run beside you as well. So your needs are not so different from those of basic obedience, but there are some marked differences from formal, or competition, obedience. The sport of agility uses obedience in its own less structured way. Let's look briefly at agility's use of a few basic tricks and commands.

Help your dog learn to love being handled by the collar.

COLLAR WORK

You will need to direct your dog by handling his agility collar sometimes, so he needs to have no aversion to your taking hold of it. You don't want to frighten him, so it's good to practice some collar games so he becomes used to this type of handling.

Just as you can teach your dog to love his leash by having him associate it with things he already loves, you can teach him to love his agility collar and your handling him by it. As soon as he is happy wearing his collar, begin touching the collar just prior to granting any of your dog's favorite wishes. Depending on how your dog feels about all of this, increase the pressure and movement you apply via his collar just before you reward him. If you're using a clicker, be sure to click as you are handling the collar and then issue the reward. The goal is to be able to take the dog by the collar whenever you need to guide or restrain him, without his losing confidence or concentration. I work my dogs up to rude collar manhandling, which they consider a playful game, so when I stretch a hand toward the collar, they throw themselves at me rather than pull away. This is beneficial in that it allows me to take hold and restrain them even when their adrenaline is pumping hard.

PICK-UP

This simple trick, known as a pick-up, is a beginner's skill that can ultimately win you a national championship. You will never be done perfecting your dog's pick-up skills. Think of your pick-up as a target game, showing the dog your outstretched index finger as a cue for him to rush directly to it in the straightest line possible. Later, on course, this cue is often accompanied by the command "Here!" It is a wonderful way to tighten up (that is, shorten) the dog's path.

I teach pick-ups as a simple clicker trick in my beginner classes. It starts as a "touch the finger with your nose" task, and the click is simultaneous with the touch. Don't worry, the dog won't go through his career ramming your finger with his nose. This is only step one. In step one, you will be stationary and moving your finger vertically beside the dog's muzzle to attract his attention. Click just before he touches it to let him know that the finger is a "good thing." As you up the ante (step two), even in your first session, you will need to click the actual touch.

The pick-up is a valuable tool for directing your dog's movement.

In step two you need to inspire your dog to volunteer to move in order to touch the finger with his nose. If you are clicking exactly as he touches and then rewarding him with a treat immediately after that, your dog will quickly be in the game.

Step three requires the dog to recognize the cue from farther away. To inspire this, I have the handler turn sideways to the dog rather than face him.

In step four the handler runs away from the dog, and the dog has to catch up with the finger on the run. The finger is presented at the handler's side, and the handler's face is turned slightly to the same side so the dog recognizes to which side he should go. This prevents many a misunderstanding later on! The handler's running helps the dog speed up. Again, the handler must click at the instant the dog touches the finger, because that is still the winning behavior at this point. After the click, the dog gets a treat.

All of these pick-up steps are covered in my beginner class, so the dog and handler have a "focus here" cue to take to the more challenging levels ahead, where the dog will have more freedom and responsibility as he begins to run sequences.

COME

Any dog that will have the privilege of being unrestrained needs to understand and obey when his handler calls him to come. Anything less is unsafe. In dog obedience competition, "Come" often denotes a specific formal exercise in which the dog is expected to come straight to the handler's front and sit facing him. In agility you want the dog to come immediately to you, but you do not want him to sit and you do not want him to cut in front of you. It's most likely that you will need him to come to one side or the other, parallel to you.

It is important to remember that the two sports, obedience and agility, require different actions for the come command. If your dog has been taught that the command means to come straight to the front and sit, then use "Here" or any other word to call your dog to you in the context of agility. If your dog has not been taught the formal obedience exercise, you might use "Come" for agility or use two different words, depending on to which side he should come (e.g., "Close" for the left side and "Side" for the right side). I use "Here" along with a pick-up finger on the side where I want the dog. My dogs love their pick-ups, so teaching a recall is just an extension of that. I add the verbal "Come" command any time after step three in the pick-up process.

Teaching your dog to come to you on command is covered at length in many training books. Just a gentle reminder: the dog needs to learn that he will be well received on arrival, so never call him to you to punish him. The dog should be greeted with a reward on arrival for many repetitions. Refinements come later.

If your dog is "selectively deaf" when outdoors, practice the recall first on a 6-foot leash, giving an appropriate reward each time, and graduate to longer lines until your dog comes charging to your call without any tension on the line, even if he is distracted.

You'll be amazed at how your dog can turn on a dime once he is reliably trained to be tuned in to you. Using the pick-up is especially useful because it is a physical cue unlike any other. Praise your dog as he hurries to catch you. In addition to the finger touch and click/treat, a few seconds of active playtime is a perfect reward for coming when called.

SIT

Sit is a good ready position that is easy to teach, easy to enforce and conducive to your dog's paying attention. You have probably already taught your

A treat, happy praise, a toy—anything desirable to the dog—should greet him when he responds to your "come" command.

dog to sit, perhaps by holding up a cookie. This enticement approach is best known to owners and well loved by most dogs. Hold the enticement at the dog's eye level, then raise it over his head as you say "Sit." Clicker trainers will click at the instant the dog's rear hits the floor, then give the treat. Make sure your order of events is clean! Click first and then treat to mark the winning behavior.

There is a good use for the sit command in agility, but if overused when introducing obstacles, it can easily become a command that saps the dog's enthusiasm. Rather than order the beginner dog to sit and stay put, thereby having to correct him and replace him whenever he moves, I like to see dogs straining to give the new obstacle a try. When introducing weave poles, tunnels and early jump sequences off leash, it's much better to have the dog eager and thinking of dynamics rather than having to concentrate on staying still. In fact, a good handler will try to jolly the dog up before he's called, making sure he's eager to go. The handler holds the dog at the ready in a forward-motivating way.

Begin by practicing the sit command away from the obstacles. Don't use it in conjunction with your dog's first introductory work. Remember, you'll have much more fun in agility if you err on the side of that energetic forward drive.

DOWN

In agility, dogs must lie down (or sit in the AKC version) on the pause table for a five-second count at any point during the course run. The count won't start until the dog assumes the correct position, and it stops if he begins to rise, so he needs to be quick and steady on the down yet maintain his enthusiasm for the rest of the run.

Training for the "instant down" is done in two steps. The first is to have the dog understand and accept the command. The second step is to have the dog throw himself into the position quickly, which requires that you use his favorite motivators.

Here's my favorite way to help dogs of any age and size love the down command (see photo on page 52). First I hold the clicker in my left hand and the reward in my right hand. I sit or kneel on the carpet and bend my left knee to form an arch. I reach under that knee with the enticement (food or toy) and invite the dog to come and get it. When he lowers himself under the knee (following the treat), I click the clicker and then give him the prize. Big party! Again, don't apply a name to the act until he is happy to do it.

As the dog anticipates this follow-the-lure game, he begins to pounce down before you kneel, leading to a straight-legged human position and the demanding "hey, click this!" down behavior that you want. Associate the down command with your dog's

As the dog goes through the "arch" formed by the handler's leg, he lowers himself into the down position and receives a click and reward.

favorite things, as you would with other commands. Take advantage of how well you know your dog. Make his favorite things contingent on the down command. You need to help him train you to give him his reward quickly. The second he's down, click the clicker and make the reward happen. The faster he's down, the faster he wins.

Try not to practice the down exercise on the agility table until your dog can do the down instantaneously, because if he puts it all together while he's still slow, he will be patterned for a slow down with the pause. Play your "instant down" games with the clicker until your dog is throwing himself down in anticipation of impressing you, and then bring that same game to the pause table.

WAIT

Everyone benefits from wait training. It has many applications at home and in agility. Canines are not designed to choose delayed reinforcement, yet it's the basis of living with humans. They have to learn to refrain from many natural things, and they have to wait for us many times a day. That's a dog's life. When you teach your dog to wait gracefully, you are helping minimize the stress of waiting. You will use this command often in agility, during early training on the obstacles and, ultimately, on the start line and pause table.

Mealtime lends itself well to wait training. Simply hold your dog's leash or collar and tell him to "Wait" as you put the dish down for him. Then you must prevent him from getting to the food until he stops trying to get it. It's a catch-22 for him, but as long as his efforts to get the food in spite of you are thwarted, he'll soon learn that when you say "Wait" he must not go forward.

You could practice this several times a day with treats or toys, telling your dog to "Wait" as you place the prize on the floor and then restrain him with the collar or leash until he stops lunging for it. When he's truly waiting, you can click and then send him to "Get it!"

RUN WITH ME!

When running with you, the dog should keep pace close at your side without interfering with your motion. Teaching him to travel short distances this way will help prevent him from taking obstacles out of proper sequence in tricky sections of an agility course. Naturally you don't want him to lag or feel put upon by this command, nor do you want to trip over him. He needs to pay attention, but you don't want him craning to look at your face. You don't want him overly dependent and you don't want him to sit, as you'll be sending him off again right away. If your dog is obedience trained to another set of specifications, you may want to use a different word for this skill in agility.

I use my pick-up game when I'm teaching my dog to run with me. Just call your dog to you and take a brisk step or two "on the finger." You might click on the first side-by-side step, depending on how difficult it is for him. Make sure you click while you are both in forward motion, which is the winning behavior you want to mark. Beware of marking stopping or sitting. That's not the behavior you're training here. Click while moving forward in tandem, even if you plan to take only one step. Click, then offer the treat, at which point you may stop to celebrate. This exercise can be done on leash at first. You don't need to argue over whether the dog will stay near you. This must be taught as a game in order to get what you want from it, which is brisk and happy tandem running.

As long as you keep these "on-the-finger" jaunts short and lively, your dog will be running beside you for several long strides within a week. That's what you need!

Once the lessons are learned at home, you need to introduce more distracting circumstances, such as quick changes of direction. An agility dog needs to toe a fine line, paying attention yet being aware of his surroundings. So keep your sessions short, active, happy and to the point.

INTRODUCTORY EQUIPMENT

Any job is easier when you use the right equipment. Here is a simple list of items you should have for your dog before you start on the obstacles:

1. A clicker. If your clicking is not "clean," that is, if you find yourself apt to click while you are moving

the enticement rather than before you move it, then please do your homework to clean up your technique. Good clicking teaches the dog to focus forward on his work and listen for the click. Bad (I call it "muddy") clicking teaches the dog to watch the food. A well-trained clicker dog does not try to get the food directly. Even with the food in the hand near him, he plans to work for it rather than steal it. His behavior says "click this!" When he hears the click, he expects a treat to follow. Get it?

2. A wide, flat collar. Your agility collar is not a choke collar, but some dogs also need a choke collar, which is used when they are not on the obstacles.

3. A sturdy leash, 4 to 6 feet long, ideally with no loop. This leash is not for pulling the dog around, but is for eliminating the option of running off. This allows you to praise your dog's success while ensuring it. Loops look innocent enough but can get caught on equipment and snag the dog. Even knots in the leash are to be avoided for safety's sake. Leather or canvas leashes are good choices. Nylon has the advantage and the disadvantage of being slippery. It slides easily through the equipment and sheds water but can be hard on the hands.

4. A short tab leash with no loop. This leash is for close work and for more advanced dogs who need less guidance less often.

5. Enticements. Use a favorite toy, food treats or whatever your dog loves. The value of enticement is in preventing and alleviating stress. As the dog becomes proficient, the enticement shifts from lure to reward, that is, from before and during the work to after the work. When you use food lures, use very small pieces. Your dog should consume the treat in the time it takes you to say "what a good dog." If you use hard biscuits, break them into small tidbits. Soft treats like cheese are better. You want to augment learning with treats. You don't need to

Alternative Equipment

The following easy-to-find substitutes will not be the quality of regulation equipment, and it's your responsibility to keep dogs and people safe when working with them. With that in mind, here are some backyard items that can be put to work:

• Hula hoops, tires, swim rings
• Cinder blocks, bricks, blocks of wood
• Boxes, barrels
• Scraps of plywood, planks, doors
• Ladders
• Bales of hay
• Tarps, old sheets, plastic or fabric remnants
• Sawhorses
• Woodpiles, fallen logs
• Picnic tables, benches
• Chairs, card tables, coffee tables
• Leaves, hills, rocks, branches
• Dowels, tubing, poles, reflector stakes
• Chicken wire, snow fencing, exercise pens
• Playground equipment

You name it! Invent your own challenges tailored to you and your dog.

teach eating. It's wise to keep a few different kinds of treats in your bait bag and mix them up.

Some of the best early agility training can be done with items you have around your home. This makeshift stuff can give you a whole new way of looking around you— agility eyes!—and your creations can be the basis for lots of fun for you and your dog. If you become interested in competition, you'll be well on your way to proficiency on any regulation apparatus and you won't be unnerved by variations in equipment from one trial to the next.

Please keep your mind on safety as you evaluate any materials. Check them thoroughly for anything that could harm the dog, and don't let them be used without removing potential hazards. It only takes a second for an accident to happen, and nearly all safety-related accidents are preventable.

Regulation equipment is not cheap, but it has been well-tested for the safety of both the dogs and the handlers. Even if you choose not to use them, you should make yourself familiar with the design of regulation obstacles.

The first agility obstacles you should make at home are tunnels and A-frames. Each builds different skills and each is easily adapted to assure the quick success of any dog. Those who find agility delightful in itself are soon well prepared for agility classes on regulation equipment. In the meantime, these homemade obstacles provide interesting opportunities for rounding out the basic education our dogs all deserve. Here are a few ideas—there are many more—about introducing agility skills in your own backyard.

A homemade tunnel can be fashioned from just about anything; the more variety you introduce, the better. Just remember to design a first tunnel that will allow your dog to succeed easily. Begin with a wide, short length of material. Some dogs, for example, are extremely wary of standard agility tunnels, so for them you could place boards or padding on the walking surface at first or start with an entirely different type of tunnel. In my classes we have hula hoops and wrapped motorcycle tires to substitute for tunnels while the dog is learning to put his body through.

With the regulation tunnels, some dogs want their owners right at the exit, and some need to see clearly the light at the end of the tunnel, which requires the owners to back up a bit. Let an assistant hold your dog at one end while you go to the other, and use an irresistible enticement to make sure that the first tunnel experience is a good one. Don't worry if your dog's actions need modification at first. It is not a predictor of difficulty later; it just means he's a thinker who needs to process new stimuli. Be patient and celebrate each milestone, and your dog may well surprise you once he gets going.

Along with teaching your dog to go through an aperture, you can also be developing his confidence about going up and over things. As for an A-frame in the backyard, the first inclines should be wide and low. Picnic benches, then picnic tables, make great A-frame supports, especially if you only have one side's worth of lumber. He can go up and down the same plank, using the top of the bench or table to turn around. The platform at the top also affords a sense of security. Soon he'll be running the plank, which is what we want. Full-charging confidence is a prerequisite to attempting a higher apex.

Don't try narrow ramps until your dog is confident on wide ones. A ladder can teach your dog a lot about walking on narrow planks. Just lay it on the ground and entice your dog to step between the rungs. This is a good way to help him practice coordinating four feet at once in a narrow space.

In general, you need to use wider footing first and progress to more narrow. Gradually build your dog's nimble expertise from low heights to steeper inclines and greater heights. If you want to teach your dog to run the ramps from the beginning (I do not do this, but many good trainers do), you can use hoops or other tricks to help your dog learn to go all the way to the end of your backyard equipment's imaginary contact zones (see Step 3 of A-frame training, Ch. 7). Good habits can be developed early on.

The initial task is not to force the dog over the equipment. The real task is to first design a challenge that he can accomplish and feel proud of and to build on that success with further challenges that increase gradually in difficulty. You are not only your dog's teacher. In your role as handler, you are challenged to motivate and inspire your dog's best and fastest work.

MAX, A REAL SUCCESS STORY
BY **BRENDA BRUJA**

Max first arrived on the scene with her mixed-breed pups at a local animal shelter. Little did she know in her abused and confused state that she would be so fortunate and live to have so much fun. Not long after Max and her pups were admitted to the shelter, my phone was ringing. I was asked if I would be able to serve as a foster parent for several weeks. The timing was perfect since I had the rest of the summer free, so off I went with leash and crate in hand!

Max was about one and a half years old, too young to be a mother, and she had been neglected, and worse, for most of her life. At the time she was brought to the shelter, she was nursing eight five-week old pups, which were draining the last drops of health from her fragile body. Max herself was a sorry sight, malnourished with protruding bones, many skin lesions from a nasty fungal infection, scars on her face, both ears badly infected and a painfully engorged udder.

Her adoption profile did not create a pretty picture. First and foremost, she was a Pit Bull. Fortunately for Max, the Cocheco Valley Humane Society does not automatically euthanize Pit Bull-type dogs, as is the policy of many shelters these days. In addition to her breed type, Max had serious health problems, she was not spayed and she was not housebroken. With her sparse coat of hair, infected skin and general poor health, the tough climate of New Hampshire often left her shaking with cold. Her chances for adoption after the pups were weaned were questionable at best. But for the next several weeks, Max and her pups would live a life of luxury with me as their full-time caretaker. I was ready, willing and able to give them healthy food, a home in the country, wood piles to play on and agility obstacles!

Max's ticket to freedom was her adorable personality and rock-solid temperament. When I approached her kennel run, she seemed as leery as any nursing bitch would be in an unfamiliar place surrounded by strangers. Within the hour, she was riding up front with me, nearly on my lap and grinning from ear to ear as we made the trip home. Max proved to be trustworthy around both people and other animals. This fun-loving creature even smiled when greeting people, which unnerved those unfamiliar with what to her was really a submissive gesture!

During her first weeks with me, Max showed me her agility daily. Despite her poor physical condition and heavy udder, she would easily scale the 4-foot-high puppy pen to nurse and care for her pups, only to exit the same way when her work was done. Running out in the field with the older dogs, Max sprung off in a dead run, then turned instantly around to race off in another direction, to the dismay of my long-striding German Shepherds in pursuit! Often in play she would jump over other dogs that got in her way. With my interest in agility nearing obsession, I became very excited about this odd-looking dog that so innocently worked her way into my heart. I was soon to find out that this was Max's nature, pure and simple and full of zest.

Long before her official adoption, I knew deep down that I would find the time and space for this dog in my life. I began introducing Max to simple agility obstacles and jumps. Max's love of food only aided her rapid progress as she tore through tunnels and strutted over ramps to receive her rewards. Max showed herself as a natural jumper, a definite plus when considering agility competition. And competition had crossed my mind only a few hundred times! Soon we were working on regulation equipment and preparing for future trials.

Max's condition was improving, so I began to challenge her more, especially in jumping, since she had such talent for it. I wasn't concerned with height, since she measured 20 inches at the shoulder, meaning that she would only be required to jump 21 inches in US competition. She had the ability to jump much higher. We began to practice on multiple jumps in alignment before moving on to jumps situated at right angles to each other. This proved to be more difficult, since jumping ability is only part of what a dog needs to suceed. Training her to accept direction would be the real challenge. The tire jump proved useful in teaching her accuracy, since she had to jump through an exact area instead of cutting corners as she had on the bar jumps. The concept of the broad jump took only a few progressions, using a tennis ball for motivation.

To Max, ramps were just a part of the scenery, and she showed no fear or hesitation on the dogwalk, crossover or seesaw. This is very unusual. Her first experience on the seesaw was on her own, as she explored the ramp in search of leftover food. The board went crashing down with a bang. No problem! It ended without a mishap but surely could have had detrimental effects on her training had she been frightened or injured herself!

Though Max and I still have a way to go in our agility training, she has come a long way.* Now healthy and housebroken, Max passed her American Kennel Club Canine Good Citizen® test and is working toward other obedience titles. She now "earns her keep" as a demonstration dog in the evening obedience classes I teach each week. Despite her unfortunate past, I feel I'm the lucky one to have found a dog like Max. She's taught me to meet life's obstacles with zest and a smile.

Note: In April 1990, Max and Brenda won the New England Regional qualifier in the Pedigree Grand Prix of Dog Agility. In August 1990, they made it to the national finals, just one year after Brenda brought Max home.

CHAPTER 3

Elements of Agility

STRENGTH AND FITNESS

Physical fitness, at least in regard to the dog, is an important part of agility. If you are interested in competition, mental fitness becomes equally important, and your own mental fitness can be more important than your dog's. In this section I will concentrate on your dog's physical strength and how to improve it. The discipline and satisfaction that will accompany the increase in strength are the foundations for mental agility fitness as well.

> Today I worked with what I had, and longed for nothing more; and what had seemed like only weeds were flowers at my door. Today I loved a little more, complained a little less; and in the giving of myself, forgot my weariness.
> —from *Today I Smiled,* author unknown

As a universal first step, there is nothing like a good brisk walk to revitalize the mind and body when you're feeling out of shape or out of touch. The more accustomed you and your dog are to getting up and around together, the less it takes to make a difference. But don't take on the rigors of an agility course with a dog that is overweight or unused to exerting himself. It is foolish to begin jump training, for example, with a dog that cannot spring up from a prone position on the floor.

A dog doesn't have to be big or heavy to be strong in the context of fitness; indeed, agility would not be the competitive sport of choice for a dog who is massive or musclebound. We want the agility dog strong enough to carry his weight effortlessly. The dog who is fit enough to run full speed every which way on a course of about 10,000 square feet in size, balancing, twisting, turning, climbing, ducking and jumping the whole time, is a strong dog. A healthy dog can accomplish some degree of physical exertion, but it takes an athletic dog to perform well at regulation agility.

Your dog's strength and stamina are what will keep him fast and able on an agility course in spite of one obstacle after another. And just as you improve the dog's ability one step at a time, you can build his strength and fitness that way. Jogging is wonderful for him. Inspect his feet as carefully as you inspect your agility obstacles. Trotting over rough or hot road surfaces can be as bad for him as splinters in your equipment. His lungs and muscles will need gradual acclimation to toughen them up, and so will his feet. If your dog leads a soft-footed lifestyle, you may need to help him develop tougher pads as you condition him. There are several salves for strengthening the calluses of dogs' feet that are available from sporting-dog catalogs and stores. Protecta-Pad is one such preparation and Tuff-Foot is another.

Any conditioning program you choose for your dog needs to consist of a combination of diet and exercise. You could switch an overweight dog to one

"Agility" might not spring to mind when looking at the Sussex Spaniel, with his short legs and long back, but a dog of any breed in good condition can be an agility candidate.

of the "light" foods initially, but it's best to settle on one of the top-quality dog foods. There really are some excellent dog foods available now, and with a little research on your part, you can find one that agrees with your dog in every way. This is a far cry from the world of generic feeds. Look for quality ingredients.

For overweight dogs, try feeding the dog about one-third fewer calories per day with a first-rate food. If you can stand it, get rid of those junk-food treats, or at least use them very sparingly. Some eager eaters happily accept nuggets of their regular dog food as treats, especially if you sprinkle them with garlic powder. Dogs love garlic, and it can be beneficial to dogs in moderation. Save empty garlic powder jars for treat storage, because the smell stays strong a long while, and they're a good size for tucking in a pocket. Just remember that treats are calories, too. The handfuls you might feed your dog

It's easy to envision a dog like the Italian Greyhound, with his lean frame, free action and sleek lines, racing through the agility course with ease.

throughout the day should be part of his calorie allotment.

Another easy way to cut down on your dog's calories is to give smaller pieces of treats. Many dogs swallow their delectable treats so fast that they don't even taste them anyway. It would help the cause for you to break that small biscuit in half or just offer a little piece of hot dog. I know people who are feeding their dogs several hot dogs a day in the name of training. That's a huge amount of unhealthy food. Spoil your dog with fun, use healthy treats and offer only a very occasional bit of junk.

Along with watching calories, gradually begin introducing more exercise every day. For a dog who is at a good weight and just needs strengthening, you don't need to lower his daily calorie intake, but you still should evaluate his diet and change some of your habits regarding treats and exercise. And be aware that whether your dog starts out fat or thin, when he has worked up to a rigorous schedule of exercise, you may need to up the amount of daily calories. Once you get your dog's weight where you want it, you can monitor it and adjust his daily intake without undue concern.

To check your dog's weight, rely on your eyes and fingers as well as the scale. Your dog carries a certain build, either large or small, wide-chested or narrow, big-boned or fine and anything in between. Most dogs are at a good weight if their ribs are not conspicuous but are easily felt with the fingers. You can see from the length of spine on a Dachshund or a Bassett Hound that extra weight will translate to back trouble. Some breeds, like the Greyhound, Saluki, Whippet and a few others, are healthiest at thinner weights. You can see from their fine, frail-looking bones that excess weight is a mistake for them.

Begin a conditioning program by looking objectively at your pet, his coat, his skin, his energy, his weight, etc. If you opt to change his food, do so by gradually decreasing the portion of his current food and adding in increasing amounts of the new food; this will help to avoid digestive upset. It's prudent to allow a week of changeover mixing for every year that your dog has had a steady diet of the old food.

Likewise, it's sensible to introduce your dog to more physical exercise both gradually and in a way he will enjoy. My favorite is walking through the woods. As the dog gets more active, and as he learns to come when you call (you're practicing your pick-ups, right?), you can give him more freedom on these walks. The running uphill and down, the change of footing from leaves to dirt to mud to water, the jumping over and ducking under things, the pushing through branches and the general charging around will do a lot for preparing your dog for agility.

Once your dog is at reasonable weight and strength, you can further condition him and

The joy of agility is unmistakable on the smiling face of this Beagle as he emerges from an open tunnel.

lengthen his stride by teaching him to trot for longer and longer distances. The trot is the gait that will do his cardiovascular and muscular systems the most good. A brisk but relaxed trot works the whole body evenly without undue strain. This is the choice for overall conditioning.

EXTRA EXERTION EXERCISES

After your dog is lean and strong, it's time to add extra exertion exercises (EEEs) to his training a few times per week. Think of these activities as more and more strenuous; they need not be everyday events.

If you have a short-legged dog, a snappy walking stride on your part may be enough to get him trotting right out, extending each leg and strengthening lungs and muscles. But be advised that very small dogs are not going to be able to run a competition agility course under the standard course time (SCT) unless they really run, not just trot. So once your little dog is up to strength overall, adding EEEs to his workouts periodically will be essential.

Extra exertion exercises are a personal thing, designed by you to condition your dog for repeated bursts of extra effort without tiring. For small dogs, an average staircase or a small steep hill in the backyard can provide the extra workout you both need. Another great EEE for small dogs, perfect for both of you to do together, is all-out running on the flat. Work up to sprints of at least 100 yards (one football field). Competition agility courses usually range between 160 and 200 yards. Add twists and turns to help your dog keep track of you while running, and switch to riding a bike (mountain bikes are perfect) to get him going faster when he's ready.

With larger dogs, you need something to help you go faster as soon as your dog is ready to work at a brisk trot. Cross-country skiing is perfect in the winter, and bicycles are great in the summer. There are attachments that will secure your dog to the bike for extended trot workouts. Mountain bikes, with their wider tires and smaller wheels and frames, are also good for exercising your dog. A speed of 8 mph for smaller dogs and 10 mph for larger dogs is a general guideline, though some dogs can work up to 12 mph. Many dogs need a few weeks' practice before they are comfortable at that speed for a considerable distance. Make adjustments based on your dog.

EEEs for strong dogs include lots of hiking, running, skiing (i.e., cross-country), playing and enjoying their fitness. Mountain biking off leash is wonderful for exercising an experienced dog, as is running in very loose, soft dirt. Steep hills and long staircases can make terrific training grounds (stadium steps are perfect for both of you). If your dog likes to chase and retrieve, he can be sent up hills and steps repeatedly and have lots of fun while exerting himself. This strategy becomes an important part of good agility handling for competition. Always throw uphill. There is too much strain on the dog's front end as he tries to scoop up his toy and turn back while running downhill. You could also teach your dog to pull a weight behind him like sled dogs do.

Group play among friendly dogs is great for dogs' muscles and social skills. A hearty romp with friends can be the perfect EEE for any dog. Once your dog is trained to come when called, you can punctuate his play sessions with recalls for treats, then say "Okay" and let him rejoin the group. If you find that your dog goes "deaf" when involved in group play, you have an opportunity to improve his training by putting a long line on him before playtime.

There are many other activities that can put you and your dog on the active track together. Backpacking and hiking over every kind of terrain are wonderful, and swimming is as good for dogs as it is for people. There are lots of great games that can keep canines in shape, including fetch, Frisbee, keep-away, tag, ball games, lure coursing, dog-sledding, skijoring and any other sport you and your dog can enjoy. My dog Spring swims for miles at a time in our 1-acre pond, playing her version of water soccer with a 10-inch plastic ball. Many dogs like to chase a rowboat, while others love a run at the beach or a jog around the city park. Whatever your environment offers, there is opportunity for strengthening your dog. There is certainly an activity you enjoy that can include your dog, and that pastime will help you both in agility.

FLEXIBILITY—MENTAL AND PHYSICAL

Mental and physical flexibility are both required in agility. Mentally, both handler and dog need to learn to welcome the unexpected. That does not come naturally to many dogs or to many people, but it is a mindset well worth developing. It's the only way to take in stride the inevitable variations in agility course design, obstacle construction, color, texture, terrain and footing, crowd and judge proximity, weather, lighting, noise, traffic, distractions near the ring, etc.

Agility would not be as exciting and interesting if we concentrated on eliminating the many individual differences our competitions have to offer. It's important to observe the standards described by the regulations, as they provide for safe course layout and equipment generally familiar to all. Without these guidelines, it would be hopeless for one club to compete with another. But within the framework of the regulations, a good deal of variation is a plus for agility.

If you don't want the sport to become a perfunctory examination of a dog's rote training, you need to keep an open mind about the eccentricities of another group's equipment and choice of trial site. Each unfamiliarity offers a new opportunity to expand the dog's experience. To prepare for the unexpected, make it your practice to work and play in so many different environments that a variation on the theme is easily handled by your solid core of mental flexibility. Welcome distraction and work to become more fun than the environment.

Physical flexibility is required in running any course in which jumps and turns are called for in quick succession and especially for performing the weave poles. Teaching physical flexibility means teaching the dog to bend vertically and laterally. Vertical bending can be taught with small tunnels and any other archways, including your bent knees as you sit on the floor. Some dogs not used to this may resist any opening requiring them to duck. Many such dogs, when first inspired to try going through, will actually put their heads into the aperture and become frustrated when their shoulders bang against the upper lip.

One way to develop this skill is to teach your dog the instant down (see Ch. 2). This will greatly enhance his vertical flexibility, as will teaching him to spring up quickly from a prone position on the floor.

Just as you should stretch out your own back by bending forward before working out, so should you accustom your dog to bending his head down to the ground to stretch his back lengthwise. I begin by using a cookie between the front legs. Bring your cookie hand in from behind the leg and invite your dog to "Get it." I teach my dogs a signal such as the one I taught my horses to lower their heads on cue. I touch behind their ears with my index finger and thumb and shape the behavior of dropping the head between the knees (I use a clicker for teaching this as a trick, of course).

Lateral bending (side to side) is practiced whenever the muscles over the dog's ribcage are compressed on one side and stretched on the other. When dogs play keep-away, tag or any game requiring them to turn, twist or run in circles, they improve their lateral flexibility. You can help your

The weave poles test a dog's lateral flexibility.

dog learn to bend this way by using an enticement to lead him around your leg. As the dog eats the treat or grabs the toy, put gentle pressure on his side with your leg, which flexes his ribcage slightly. For very small dogs, you can do the same thing kneeling down, using your knee.

Once your dog is used to your bending him gently, you can teach him to bend himself a little farther. You should not force his body yourself. Just use your hand to brace his flanks against your leg, and lead his front end around with a treat or toy. Like any other training, you should set him up to succeed easily at first. Lead him to bend just a little, mark his cooperation with a click or just say "Good" as he bends and then let him have the enticement. The dog controls his own front end and thus the amount of flex. Your part is to steady his hind end and encourage him with your voice and the reward. Repeat the bending a couple of times on each side.

You may find that your dog bends better in one direction than in the other. Most of us do. Some dogs also have a strong preference for turning and circling in one direction. You can help develop his flexibility by practicing quick spins and turns to both sides, especially his weaker one, using an enticement or playfulness. The rule of thumb is to do twice as many reps on the weaker side as you do on the stronger side. Though he may always have a better side, your dog will need to be comfortable turning and bending in both directions for agility.

You also help your dog learn to flex his body when you teach him to weave through the agility weave poles. Competition weave poles are close together and require a good deal of concentration in addition to physical flexibility, so they are best taught in several steps (see Ch. 10), incorporating a positive introduction to both controlled lateral bending and mental effort.

CONTROL

Successful completion of an agility course requires that your dog come when called, jump, stay, go up an incline, lie down, weave and go through an aperture—all on command. That's a lot of control. The dog must tackle these challenges in the unpredictable required order called by his handler, often resisting his preference for a favorite obstacle and performing the one next to it on his handler's command. To be sure, the dog must be under control. But don't make control a dirty word. Mere compliance without delight does not do justice to the sport and spirit of agility.

A nice way to help your dog accept control with pleasure is to devise a game that allows him to train himself. Not unlike many of us, a dog learns best what he discovers for himself. If you'd like an easy way to introduce a little positive control into your dog's daily life, try playing "no free lunch." Before you do something that the dog wants and expects, such as opening the door, putting down the dinner bowl or attaching a leash, ask the dog to perform a command. However, don't ask for the same behavior each time. Mix it up so he must listen and sort the task, not just develop a ritual. Control on the agility course needs to be conceptual, not ritualized.

Do you have more than one dog? You can play a great control game called "treats in turn." Get a handful of treats and call the dogs. When they've assembled around you and are giving you their undivided attention, say one dog's name, then offer a treat directly to that dog's mouth. Any interference from another dog must be intercepted calmly and not reinforced. Next, say another dog's name and follow immediately with a treat to that dog. Only the dog whose name is spoken is eligible for a treat. If that dog jumps for the treat, just move your hand back and say nothing. When he has all feet on the floor again, move the treat to his mouth again.

The pause table is perhaps the most difficult agility exercise of all in that it is a true test of control for both dog and handler.

Don't make him lose a turn; he is just insecure about who will get the treat. He'll quickly relax and be patient because he will see how it works and know that he can trust you. The emphasis is on the dog's tuning in for his name and accepting a treat in turn. There is no need to combine this exercise with the command to sit, because in agility we don't want the dog to sit every time he pays attention. It's okay if they choose to sit, but don't require it. The focus is on patience and trust. The beauty of this game is in the wonderful pack lessons taught quietly and under your control. This game quickly teaches the group that whenever you need their attention they can assemble politely to watch, listen and wait for you to notice and reward them. This kind of control, using your quiet self-assurance and the good stuff the dogs desire, is extremely helpful to a harmonious family life. It has a great deal of positive transfer to the chaotic world of agility trials as well.

This lesson of taking turns is hardest on your leader dog, who must learn to watch food go past him to his underlings. Use your body to interrupt any rudeness, but make it a quiet lesson. There is no need to become impatient with the dogs' impatience. They will learn patience from your authority and from your calm, precise technique. It's your attitude and quiet warding off of bad manners that will make the dogs accept the sharing situation. You must not give a treat to a dog that is being impolite or out of turn. It doesn't take more than a few one- to two-minute sessions for all the dogs to get the idea and enjoy the control game. It helps youngsters learn each others' names, too.

One of the most common control problems facing dog owners is how to handle the game of "catch-me-if-you-can." It's not a bad game, but play only with your dog on leash or long line until he understands how to stop playing on cue. You can intersperse the game with recalls and instant downs (Ch. 2) to help him give up his advantage when you ask him to. I do enjoy playing chase games with my dogs—outside. It helps develop agility and quick reflexes while enhancing our kindred sense of fun in motion. But I don't appreciate having my dog initiate such a game when we're working on some less kinetic lesson or when I am expecting him to come to me or when I am having a quiet conversation in the living room. In my home, I have drawn the line between the game we all love and the times when we may not play it. We don't initiate the game unless we are outside and willing to play, and we don't respond to the dog's invitation to play anytime other than when we are in play mode. Over time, the dogs have learned that we act like their peers occasionally (indeed we are out of our league when we play chase with them), but that the role of peer is one we assume now and then, not one that is available to them at their whim.

Turning on a dime and off to the next obstacle! At a high level of competition, there's not a fraction of a second to lose.

It is always a direct challenge to the handler to be able to control the dog without sapping his confidence. In countries in which agility competition is still young, some correct but placid performances can be enough to win since accuracy is foremost. But for the most part, when several hundred dogs are typically entered in a day's competition, and the winners will all have clear rounds and be separated in their times by hundredths of a second, accuracy and obedience are not enough. This sheds a different light on that word *control*. Handler strategy, the dog's work ethic and enthusiasm and all of the fundamentals are tested at once, in less than a minute per dog. The dog must be fast, bold and independent, yet take instant direction from the handler's commands. That's what we want from control in agility.

The finesse is to instill in the dog navigational control from the handler and the self-control of proper obstacle performance, which can all be attended to by the dog while he is running with joy and full confidence at top speed. On the course, keeping your dog's attention without impeding his run depends on getting him to accept your instructions with zest and fire. The best control training improves your own timing and accuracy as well as your dog's. It's a two-way street.

CHAPTER 4

Teamwork—TLC

TEAMWORK—TLC

What makes a good team? What is it like to be your teammate? What does it take to get the harmony of effort, so pretty to watch, that makes the work look easy and the job go smoothly? And why do even the most solid teams, whether dancers, baseball players or agility nuts, have days when they trip over each other's feet and can't find the rapport they had only yesterday? Whatever teamwork is, it sure takes work to build it as well as to maintain it.

> "God summoned a beast from the field and He said…'I endow you with these instincts uncommon to other beasts: faithfulness, devotion and understanding surpassing those of man himself. Lest it impair your loyalty, you shall be blind to the faults of man. Lest it impair your understanding, you are denied the power of words…Speak to your master only with your mind and through honest eyes…So be silent, and be a friend to man…This shall be your destiny and your immortality.' So spake the Lord. And the dog heard and was content."
>
> —From the motto of the American Dog Owners Association

We can all recognize the special communication that sets some relationships apart from the rest. The partners respond to each other's thoughts, seemingly without a clue. You and your dog can become a more responsive working partnership if you develop the TLC of teamwork: trust, leadership and confidence. As you learn to use and coordinate these skills, they become an inextricable part of your interaction with your canine teammate. Eventually you live by the rules of TLC as naturally as you breathe, without having to concentrate on them. But you must tune in to your dog to find them, and it takes adjustment and effort to develop them. Trust, leadership and confidence are the intangibles that distinguish the finest agility performances, and they stand out just as clearly in the most harmonious human-canine bonds at home.

TRUST

The trust that evolves in a great team cannot be demanded. You must earn it, and it's a fragile thing at first, becoming stronger with the nurturing you put into it. When your dog fully trusts you, he'll give a great effort just because you ask for it. He has faith that what you ask is okay and that he can do it if you say so. Conversely, if your dog does not trust you, his positive attitude has little to sustain it when the going gets tough. Don't blame your dog for not giving a wholehearted attempt at a new task. Instead, set about earning your dog's complete trust in your daily life, and then bring that trust to bear in agility training.

Does your dog trust you? First of all, does he know you well? Your dog cannot trust you if he can't predict your reactions to the everyday situations of his life. A trusting relationship requires consistency in your household rules and corrections that your dog can understand. Dogs study the ones they live with and are masters of body language, so it is likely that your dog can read your moods. His trust depends on how those moods affect him personally. So the cornerstone of trust is predictability. Each action you take with your dog affects his ability to predict you. You must earn your dog's trust, one action at a time.

If a certain action on your part is followed by another particular action time and time again, your dog learns to predict that second action. You pick up the car keys, and he expects that you're going for a ride. You pick up his leash, and he assumes that you're going to take him for a walk. It's that predicted action, what he expects to happen next, that determines his feelings when you do what you do.

Your dog's predictions can strengthen or weaken your relationship. If you are prone to screaming at him when you arrive home for something he did during your absence, he predicts this and feels insecure when you come home. That does not mean he connects your coming home to the mistakes he made some time ago. It is much more likely that his insecurity upon your arrival is due to his prediction that an unpleasant encounter with you is coming next. He need not know why. These feelings are confusing and foster insecurity and poor self-image. They do not foster trust.

If you expect your dog to get into trouble while you are gone, teach him to sleep in a crate in a favorite spot in your home or in another safe, secure area so you can leave him alone without worrying about damage, both to your home and your relationship. Prevent unwanted behavior from happening in your absence and concentrate on improving your dog's manners when you are home. Since canines are, by nature, den animals, it is usually not difficult to help them associate the crate with comfort. You can learn a lot about positive crate training from obedience training books.

For many dogs, this is the beginning of a better relationship with humans.

It's very important that your dog is happy to see you when you come home and vice versa. If you want to trust your dog, see to it that he learns what you need him to know. He can't do it without you, and he can't trust you until you can approve of him. The job of earning his trust and his earning your trust is entirely up to you. It can be a lot of work at first, but it gets much easier as you keep at it. So get to know your dog and learn to bring out the best in him.

You have already earned an important type of trust from your dog if you are reliable about seeing to his basic needs, including food, water, grooming, exercise and love. Those come first. Then, to develop a stronger bond, teach him the manners he will need in your home. These become the ground rules between the both of you. Without them, neither of you can trust the other because you don't know what to expect from each other.

Once you and your dog have learned to get along well in your daily life, you can further develop trust with agility play sessions on backyard equipment such as that described in Chapter 2. Your dog learns to trust your judgment as you offer him a new challenge and help him master it. Be sure you choose a time, environment and task all suited to quick success and be properly prepared with an agility collar, a leash and enticements. It's fine to assume that your dog will have no hesitation or problems with these exercises, but be ready to help at once if it doesn't turn out that way. Your dog's trust in you will be given a boost for every success you celebrate together and will be set back with every problem. One advantage to starting with simple makeshift obstacles at home is that you and your dog can build a good working relationship, which will help you progress that much faster when you get to regulation agility equipment.

When you're working with a solid foundation of trust, your bond will only be enhanced by sharing the fun and excitement of agility.

It will do your trust factor good if you introduce your dog to a challenge with you right beside him, encouraging him as necessary and using food or a toy to keep his spirits up. During these first stages, don't worry about your dog's accuracy on an agility obstacle, but do put some study and effort into your own handling technique. It's important for you to develop good training skills because they will help you establish correct agility habits in your dog early on. These skills will also help you develop your eye for safety and help you protect your dog. Your dog's trust in you will quietly grow, but be patient. You will find that you can't work on everything at once, especially when you're just starting out. Take your time and avoid putting pressure on the dog. Sit in the tunnel with him if he's uneasy. Let him lean on you while he walks up a ramp. If you are beside him, steadying him and sharing your confidence and patience, he will learn to trust you. In time he will feel that he can do anything you ask and that life is grand when he gets that chance.

Does your dog trust you? Will he tune in to you? Does he tend to settle down if you think quiet thoughts and settle down yourself? What if you massage his shoulders, thighs and legs? Will he let you handle his feet? It takes trust for a napping dog to remain relaxed while you rub his limbs and particularly while you touch his feet.

Does your dog know your touch from anyone else's? Two of my dogs will all but purr with pleasure if I touch them while they're stretched out, but their eyes will pop open to check out the same interruption from anyone outside the family. It's easy to build trust in a dog that loves everyone because he has a trusting nature to work with. You just need to take the time to let him settle himself down while you remain calm. This takes tuning in on the part of both of you.

Can you relax your dog when he's feeling nervous and insecure? That takes a higher level of trust. If he reacts with fear to something that is not dangerous, can you convince him to check it out and accept it? Start by approaching and touching the new thing (or person) yourself, then put that hand on your dog's muzzle and then on the object again, but do not pull your dog to it. Use any enticement and encouragement to teach him, perhaps over several exposures, to approach in spite of his insecurity. Say non-threatening things like "What is that?" or "Wanna say hi?" Use your clicker or just a well-timed, quiet "good" as he takes each tiny step or reaches out his nose. Use what you know about your dog to help him keep trying when he's hesitant.

This work is not a matter of obedience *per se.* Ignore his failures. Don't force him, and don't inadvertently reward failures by petting your dog or getting out your clicker whenever he hides behind you. Try to make a tiny bit of progress and then get out the clicker as a reward for his rudimentary effort. If you manipulate the order of events carefully, soon the dog's willingness to reach out and smell the object of his uncertainty stems from his own curiosity once he trusts your judgment that all is okay.

These trust exercises will help to build your dog's faith in you. It will damage that faith if you punish him for noncompliance or inaccuracy now. First find a challenge at which he can easily succeed and use that as your starting point. You can even work on your own accuracy as a handler by practicing with a stuffed animal instead of your dog. That way, you are free to make many of the mistakes you're bound to make without having them shape bad habits in your dog.

Don't take your dog's trust for granted. The more timid dogs need to trust their owners in order to give new challenges a try. See to it that they view every attempt as a success. The more independent dogs need to trust their owners in order to take their owners' advice. See to it that they are rewarded for listening. That sounds obvious, but many handlers cause mistakes and then bring their dogs back for retries when the dogs actually did exactly as they were directed the first time. I tell my students to keep on going, because it is more important that the dog can trust his navigator.

Your dog's trust begins with basic obedience and household etiquette. He learns that you say what you mean and mean what you say. You introduce basic agility skills in a low-pressure environment, teaching the dog that the two of you are a team and can accomplish things to make you both proud. And you build upon that trust when you tackle more challenging situations, distractions and agility exercises. Your dog learns to trust you even when it's more difficult to do so.

The next level of trust requires that you never order an impossible task. It's fine to call for an effort that requires your dog to stretch his abilities a little,

Your dog's trust in you will help the two of you work through those times when the dog seems hesitant about an obstacle or stressed by some aspect of training.

either mentally or physically, but don't ever demand what you can't help him accomplish. Above all, don't push his education too fast. Even a mature, well-trained dog occasionally needs your conservative guidance to keep him from biting off more than he can chew.

It's often tempting to skip the introductory levels of training on any one obstacle, but don't do it. The risks outweigh the benefits. Most of my agility students fall for that trap. Usually they get carried away by the dog's apparent initial confidence. They become interested in a challenge for which the dog is not fully prepared and try it anyway.

Sometimes the dog seems to take to the obstacle immediately, performing the regulation dog walk or seesaw or bar jump on the very first exposure, without working up to it. Suddenly, on the next attempt or even sessions later, the dog seems to have lost all confidence on that obstacle. Since, commendably, the handler has taught his dog to expect success, the dog often does succeed on the first try. But the stress he feels during that unprepared initial effort can create a strong negative impression of the obstacle, which soon overtakes him.

I had a wonderful Rough Collie for 13 years, and he was a very accomplished citizen by the time he was retired. When he ended his obedience career and took on the new role of chief house pet, he needed supplemental work to keep his spirits up, so he chose to help with certain chores. I took care of several farm-fuls of animals on a regular basis, and on one job I carried two five-gallon jugs of water to the chicken house every day and brought the jugs back empty. Spring was as proud as a peacock to carry an empty jug. But he wanted also to carry the jugs when they were full; it seemed all the same to him. I never told him no, but I always kept the full jugs away from him and then gave him an empty one. So I often walked to the chicken house with an elderly Collie gentleman dancing at my heels, trying to wrest a jug from this hand or that.

Friends suggested, "Why don't you just let him try, and he'll see he can't lift it?" But I felt he wouldn't trust me so completely if I let that failure happen. I knew him well enough to predict that if he grabbed a jug, expecting to hoist it and strut with it, and met absolute failure, he would not quite trust me enough to try the next new task with the same vigor. I chose never to offer him a job he couldn't do. For all his life he had expected to work and succeed, and he did so with gusto.

This was my personal judgment call, based on a long, close relationship with that individual dog. Certainly many dogs could be handled differently, but in general that philosophy has served me well. Don't give your dog a task he cannot perform, or even one that he feels he cannot do. As you get to know his weak spots, you can strengthen your dog's trust in you by improving these areas very, very gradually and by being right there beside your dog to prevent a shaky mentality from letting failure set in. And by the way, the more your dog takes his confidence from you rather than from himself, the more damage it will do to his trust in you whenever he feels insecure about your demands.

I have seen many a good handler decide to test his dog by ordering the dog to do a task more difficult than for what the dog was prepared. Sometimes the dog balks. The dog trusts his own judgment and questions that of his handler. Smart dog, I suppose, since the handler showed a lack of sense by demanding a quantum leap above the dog's level of readiness. It also leads me to expect the dog to mistrust his handler's judgment more readily in the future. Time and time again, even an excellent handler will push his dog too hard, then pay the price for weeks afterward by having to rebuild the dog's confidence to a level that they had previously surpassed. A small test can cost a good deal of the dog's trust, a heavy price.

One person I know couldn't resist testing his beloved and very talented dog on a whopping 12-foot-high arched playground ladder. He climbed up himself and straddled the top, having told his dog to wait. When he ordered her up, she sprang with all the strength of her faith in him and struggled to where he caught her by the buckle collar and helped her over the top. She had no experience climbing down such an obstacle either, but she gamely made the attempt until gravity called her to jump the last several feet. She landed safely and was congratulated and hailed a great success, but that was the last time she would consider it. He tried to repeat the feat, but she absolutely refused. That utter trust was gone.

She was that rare dog that could have learned to handle such a difficult obstacle if they had worked up to it, so I can't help but think that her owner sold that strength short. It was beautiful to see in her first try the power of her perfect faith in her owner. It seems that strong-willed people who themselves handle pressure and stress well are more apt to apply heavy pressure to their dogs than are people who are more intimidated by stress.

Your dog is not a simple creature, although his needs and demands often seem so. You shouldn't assume you always understand him. Each of us can learn from other people who tackle things differently. Study the positive thinking of adventurers if you're shy; watch the preparation of careful people if you're impatient. Balance your own natural tendencies with the inspiration of other people who show you something you admire. You will understand your dog better and develop your potential as a team if you explore many ways to look at a situation and bring home a new bit of insight with every outing. It helps you appreciate your dog and can show you new ways to help your dog really appreciate you.

LEADERSHIP

A good agility leader inspires confidence in himself while also enhancing his dog's personal confidence. He brings out his dog's strengths, heads off the dog's weaknesses and motivates his dog by word and action. His energy and confidence are contagious to his canine teammate. He exudes assurance and great expectations without making his dog a victim of high pressure.

Sound like you? Me neither, but I'm working on it. Some of us are great leaders in the classroom and in the backyard, and that's a good place to start. I have some fine students with no interest in formal competition who enjoy agility just as much as I do. Your dog doesn't need competition to complete his life. If you don't either, that's fine. Your leadership skills are still important to you and your dog.

Your more stressful challenges will arise from maintaining your leadership around distractions, without the added pressure of competition. It's challenge enough to work well with your dog on a crowded street or on a familiar agility course. It's extremely difficult to bring that talent unchanged to the nationals. There's nothing like a national title, a TV crew and several thousand spectators to test your leadership skills to the limit. Many good dog/handler teams stay home.

Like all of the intangibles, leadership has to begin at home. Daily living habits and simple obedience lessons can help your dog view you as a leader, but leadership is more than telling your dog what to do. The dog who really accepts you as leader will accept your massaging the back of his neck, hugging him, hovering over him and handling his body. It's necessary for your dog to be able to relax and enjoy these overtures from you rather than to fear or resent them as dominance gestures. Obedience and control games help your dog recognize and welcome friendly attentions from his leader.

Many dogs have adopted another dog as their leader. When the lead dog gets going, the follower wants to be right behind. Your agility dog will be a superior teammate if he is that interested in what you do. To help him relate to you as his leader, make an effort to lead him in a way he can understand. Try setting up a situation that will be interesting and fun for your dog and put you in the leader's role. Going for a ride in the car is an everyday example for some dogs. Going boating, jogging or biking are others. For dogs who love water, swimming and even watering the garden can present leadership opportunities for you.

Now and then, initiate an activity that is distinctly "doggy." Chase a squirrel with your dog and throw a stick up in the tree after it. Jump up against the tree a few times. It's important to take

This pair seems perfectly in sync as the dog looks up at his handler to follow her direction.

charge at the tree, showing command of the situation from the dog's point of view. Many dogs love to chase flies, good practice for quickening reflexes. Every now and then I invite my bug-nabbers on a fly chase. They are always quite impressed when I get a fly, and they don't seem to mind that I cheat by using a flyswatter. I also miss the best part by not eating the fly, but they know better than to raid the wastebasket for it because I'm the leader.

I have one dog who likes to watch TV, so we can enjoy animal scenes together. Dogs who love to dig should have a designated digging area, and you should be chief excavator now and then. The possibilities go on and on, guided only by your dog's favorite doggy activities.

We all know that bonding with your dog includes showing affection, but many dogs need a leader they can respect on their own terms, too. So get down and doggy sometimes. Many great canine agility prospects are dogs who don't love to be cuddled. Take a good look at your dog and let yourself relate to him as his leader in action as well as someone who pets him and feeds him.

Everybody has different goals in agility. Whatever your goals, every dog and every handler has personal character traits that make agility training a challenge. Granted, some have more than others. I prefer to look on these traits as "qualities." There is a positive side to every character trait, and it is the leader's job to develop this quality and use it to the team's advantage. My dear Rottie Jessy has a mind as hard as they come, and more than once she has disagreed with my choice of obstacle and told me so. In one competition she even pushed me aside to get to the one she preferred, thwarting my attempt to anticipate her reaction and block the tricky spot. Something like this is a humbling experience, and it short-circuits your leadership in a hurry. How can teamwork come of this? How can you feel like a leader when your dog's personal confidence seems stronger than your own?

Start by evaluating you and your dog individually. You can pinpoint many of your own motivations and habits, which will help you learn the ropes of this sport. Start by making a list. Now dig deeper and list the habits that might cause you problems in agility training. In a separate column, list the helpful characteristics that your dog brings to the partnership, including his intrinsic motivators. Then list the traits you recognize as potential problems in his agility training. It will help you design effective approaches to training if you know your strong and weak areas. And, most of all, you can see which of your traits is apt to conflict with your dog's traits. Each agility dog you train will require a separate interaction sheet. You will need to modify your approach many times in order to bring out the best in each dog and, in turn, emerge as a handler with good leadership qualities.

Your dog is who he is: a canine, a certain breed or breed mix and a particular individual. These facts determine much of his interpretation of the world, and you can't change that in a basic sense. But you can work with it. Depending on many factors, such as his age, the time and effort you invest, the quality of that time and effort, the compatibility of your approach with his personality and so on, you will be able to shape your dog's outlook and his abilities to an amazing extent.

Begin by working with your dog, not against him. For major training problems, make note of what you ultimately want and where you are now in relation to that. Then design intermediate goals, which are the steps to get from here to there. Whether this particular goal requires a few steps or many steps depends on how far from it you are. It would not be fair to your dog for you to expect things too quickly from him. A written goal sheet will help you plan and monitor your progress on a particular problem and will keep you from avoiding it. Believe me, if you bury a problem, it will surely resurface when the pressure is on.

That hard-headed independence of Jessy's became the same tough-minded persistence that took her jumping ability from inadequate to good. Along the way she worked through some tough agility challenges that would have weeded out most heavy-set dogs. Her stubborn ways could be a plus. It was up to me, because I was supposed to be the leader. If I couldn't always be smarter than she, at least I needed to be the better manager.

Years ago I kept an agility training diary to monitor the progress of young Jessy. I lasted about a month with it, and it was very useful. For the first week, the entries read like a how-to test, beginning at a logical step one and making slow but steady progress. Then came week two. The first entry announces a setback, and the next day's entry is just

"AAAAGH!!!" The following day is blank, the next day says we're going to try again and the next day reads much like step one.

It helps, especially when you're working out a snag, to keep track of your progress, uneven though it might be. You will easily see if a pattern develops and you will think more clearly with your deeds in writing. Although I haven't yet done so, I would like to keep a diary of a dog's entire training regimen for a year or more. It's impossible to remember most of the important details. Trials and errors, quirks and breakthroughs in one dog's training can provide some insight for another day, another dog or another handler.

After all, we can't be brilliant every day, and writing down our work and ideas gives us access to that much more information and experience next time. If you like to write, try keeping a diary to help you solve one training snag between you and your dog. I think you'll find it very useful, both now and later.

You should always work on simple things with the more difficult things in mind. Choose a starting point at which you both can succeed. Choose inter-mediate goals that will challenge your dog—but not too much. This philosophy will make it easier to back up a little whenever you see yourself going too fast or pushing too hard and it will help you and your dog accomplish goals that you didn't think you could reach.

Leadership is the connecting thread that is woven back and forth through the work you and your dog do together. It's an invisible thing and it doesn't remain strong without your steady efforts to enhance it. Without your attention, slowly but surely the thread loosens and begins to unravel. Look at it this way: every day your fabric gets stronger or weaker, according to your work. The best dog/handler teams, like the best marriages, have great days and terrible days. A good leader knows, and surely his dog knows just as much or even more, that the relationship is what it's all about.

CONFIDENCE

Confidence is such an elusive intangible. To do your best on an agility course you need to feel confident in yourself, in your dog and in the strong relationship between you. Your dog needs confidence in his ability and in you as his leader. Bringing out and channeling the dog's confidence is your job (as if you didn't have enough to work on just developing your own). A lapse of confidence anywhere undermines the strength of the team.

In order to develop confidence as an agility team, you need to be emotionally bonded with your dog. Without that, you can still do your pet a big favor by introducing him to agility and basic obedience, and you can use these tools to help develop his confidence and tractability. But unless you and your dog tune in to each other and find a mutual affection, you will not be able to make the most of agility.

Agility is certainly a means as well as an end. I have used agility training with more than a thousand dogs as a training aid and confidence-builder. As you embark on the first tunnel and A-frame lessons, you are beginning agility confidence work. Think of your pet being pushed and dragged

Teamwork is a beautiful thing on and off the agility course. Author Julie Daniels with (LEFT TO RIGHT): Clark, Punch and Spring.

into a regulation agility tunnel or up a steep, narrow dogwalk plank, and imagine what his first impression would feel like. For most dogs, even though they may have come to the lesson with superior aptitude for agility, a first experience based on aversion met with force is disastrous. It represents the opposite of teamwork. This approach does lasting damage to the dog's trust in you, your image as his leader and above all to his confidence.

The dog who is introduced first to a hoop or tire, then to a short tunnel and then to gentle inclines is a dog who has maximum opportunity to develop agility confidence. Praise, enticements and rewards should be lavishly enjoyed.

Some dogs get so excited over treats that they are slap-happy about details like where their feet should go, and for first introductions I prefer to permit the dog to work that way in order to cement that go-get-it positive attitude. The careful work of keeping the dog properly on the apparatus falls to the handler.

In all probability the dog who is so food-crazy that he's careless is also a dog whose confidence on the equipment is quickly assured, and then it's fine to back off a bit and have him think about his performance a little more. But no harshness from you is called for even if he's jumping up and down. Just steady him quietly and let him figure it out. Give as much guidance and enticement as the situation warrants. It's your judgment. Your dog's delight in the first lessons translates into confidence, and it's this generalized confidence that will keep you both succeeding as the lessons get more demanding.

We all know dogs who come on like maniacs, so enthused about everything that they want to charge here and there, jumping on everything and everyone. Remember that because a dog exhibits manic behavior does not necessarily mean that the dog is confident. In fact, many active dogs display an even higher level of energy when they don't know what to do. So don't rush ahead with excessively challenging obstacles with very physical dogs. Keep your own body position steady and your handling techniques in order because you won't have a lot of time to correct yourself if your crazy friend gets himself into trouble. Follow a logical progression in your work sessions and don't go on to the next level of challenge prematurely.

Many times a dog will rush through an obstacle because he lacks confidence and wants to get to the end. The dog may be carrying his tail up and his head high, seemingly showing all the confidence in the world but feeling quite unsure of himself inside. When this is the case and you respond by introducing a tougher challenge, you could be setting up a serious setback in confidence later on.

Let the dog demonstrate his acclimation to an obstacle by performing it willingly with you at his side a few times. One way to tell if the dog is rushing from lack of confidence is to have him wait partway along. The dog who is truly comfortable on the obstacle will be glad to eat a cookie or two along the way or stop for a belly rub. The dog who is manic and insecure will be quite stressed about stopping. In that case, go back to square one and develop confidence with the dog's favorite motivators at that first level, then proceed more slowly. Remember, food and toys can be used to slow your dog down as well as to speed him up and keep him in the middle.

Don't automatically assume that a crazy dog is simply one with a very high energy level. This could be the case, but hyperactivity can also indicate a medical problem, anything from a genetic imbalance or a thyroid condition to a food allergy. Certainly this type of behavior calls for investigation, along with basic education, healthy diet, proper socialization and lots of exercise.

Now is the time to begin proper training practices as a handler, especially since you're avoiding putting any stress of accuracy on the dog just yet. Practice placing your rewards correctly. For example, hold the food down low and in the middle of the plank or you'll be enticing your dog right off the incline. As you learn to stand beside your dog, extending your food arm properly and using the agility collar effectively, he is free to feel safe, happy and brave. You are fostering trust, establishing your leadership and developing confidence. Teamwork is coming.

In the further interest of long-term confidence, keep each lesson short and sweet. Don't work your dog until he is tired. End the lesson while he's still eager to do it again. That way he's sure to welcome the sight of the equipment when you come back to it. For the same reason, always control the level of difficulty in the lesson so that your dog emerges with feelings of accomplishment. By following these guidelines, practicing agility skills can turn confidence-building into pleasure for both dog and handler.

A dog who approaches the introductory agility obstacles with trepidation, tail tucked and body low, needs extra time to check out the equipment before being asked to work with it. This kind of dog can benefit from being an observer at a more outgoing dog's lessons for awhile, and he needs the opportunity to sniff everything to his heart's content. But don't assume that agility is not for this dog. Many such dogs have begun slowly and become agility nuts in time, as long as their training is conducted with their confidence always in mind. Some people do not have the patience to develop competence in this kind of dog, but lucky is the hesitant dog whose owner does.

Your dog need not be a socialite to be a good candidate for agility. Many dogs who cannot make friends easily have forged a strong bond to one special human. If you have a special dog that is

When it comes to confidence, you're as big as you feel!

undersocialized, you might be surprised how much you can do for his general confidence by adding some agility exercises to his life. As long as you are willing to be the dog's big buddy, you can develop great teamwork with that dog. As you practice and your skills improve together, your insecure friend will become confident as long as you are there to keep up his self-esteem. When you are absent, distracted or unhappy, he won't have the emotional strength to sustain his ability. He takes his confidence straight from your heart.

If your shy dog has real aptitude for agility, and isn't nasty-tempered, agility could even become a good competition sport for the two of you. No group work is required in an agility competition. You and your dog will be tested by yourselves against the course and the clock, and your dog need only go about the work at hand and ignore a nearby judge and the commotion outside the ring. If that is too much hassle for your dog to bear, you can still do his confidence a world of good by introducing agility challenges in a familiar environment. And one thing leads to another; you may one day decide that your dog is ready for gradual acclimation to the big wide world, with agility as a common denominator. This sport will surprise you. I have seen a very introverted dog jump onto a picnic table smack in the middle of lunch with a group of strangers. Picnic tables make great training aids, and this dog invited herself to hop up even though she would normally shy away from people.

Every dog has little agility gremlins that come up and grab him from time to time. They seem to hold his pasterns and make him hit the jumps or they wobble his feet on the planks and make him unsteady. Above all, they whisper in his ear that he can't do it and, with that, they toss his confidence out of his head. Dogs have different ways of communicating to us that the gremlins have taken their confidence. You can't always recognize the various ways in which your dog deals with his gremlins, so don't punish your dog for failure.

I had a very good dog who met her gremlins head on: when in doubt, barge ahead. Tackle something. It was her way. It took me a long time to figure out that she charged the equipment even harder and listened less to me when her confidence was shaky. I thought she was displaying brazen confidence and lack of teamwork. Things started going a lot more smoothly when I realized that she really needed me to slow the lesson down and review easier work until she got her confidence back.

I had another very good dog who handled things quite differently: when in doubt, circle tightly to the left. This was sometimes harder for me to bear, but at least it was easy to tell when his confidence was wavering. Again, the answer is to slow the lesson down and review an easier version of the same task.

In addition to his own gremlins, your dog can be the victim of your nerves. Your dog will be freer to feel confident if you let him feel your pride in him. Most dogs have an Achilles heel in agility, so we seldom run a complete course without holding our breath here and there, even with our teamwork well in place. Try to balance your dog's problems with positive energy. By working with an eye to the dog's confidence, you can often prevent a tough spot from breaking his concentration.

In planning your training sessions you need to think forward to your dog's personal problem spots and plan a strategy to help your pet overcome his shortcomings gradually. Succeeding quickly at a task designed to be mildly challenging for him will bolster his confidence. Pretty soon, over weeks or months of steps toward your goal, your dog will become confident about challenges that used to get the better of him. Remember, your dog needs you to work with him in mind when you train. Never mind any outside pressures to reach certain goals. You are the one who knows his weaknesses and must work gradually and patiently to overcome them. As he progresses in ability, you must still maintain control of situations that are personally difficult for your dog.

There's no way around it—the dog's confidence in himself and in you, and your confidence in yourself, your dog and the relationship between you, all falls to you. As you work at it all, you'll get to know yourself better than you ever have and you'll learn much about what makes you and your dog work harmoniously. It's worth the effort because, on those days when it all comes together, the two of you can jump the moon. That unbeatable fit is what people notice when they watch a great team. The rarity of it is what makes great teamwork shine so bright.

CHAPTER 5

Basics of Handling

SEQUENCING

"Sequencing" means completing two or more obstacles in a row. The term "run-through" is used for a practice run on a full course. Helping your dog learn the fine points and particulars of running an agility course is done by designing specific sequences to expose him to all of the tricky elements, two at a time, three at a time and so on, gradually putting it all together.

> *When love and skill work together, expect a masterpiece.*
> —John Ruskin

Sequencing helps build confidence, stamina and mental sharpness. For beginner dogs, sequences are the building blocks of course running. For experienced dogs, sequencing is the best way to set up specific challenges for extra practice. We refer to these focused sequences as "skill sets."

Sequencing ability is an obvious necessity for a dog to run through a full agility course.

I start dogs sequencing early in their agility training. As your dog's ability develops with individual agility obstacles, sooner or later he'll be ready to go from one obstacle to another before being rewarded. Don't wait until your dog is able to do all obstacles at regulation difficulty before beginning to use sequences.

Begin with two of his favorite pieces of equipment, keeping it simple at first. You could use a lowered A-frame and dog walk, for example. Design initial sequences that will introduce your dog to the feeling of completing one obstacle after another without his having to think about whether he can handle any particular obstacle you include.

A good first sequence consists of an open tunnel followed by a low jump. Since the dog expects you to play with him when he exits the tunnel, he may trip you up as you move on to the jump, he may slow down before the jump or he may appear to be refusing the jump. It's different from the pattern he's used to, so don't be upset if he balks. Coaxing him to continue on to the jump and using a strong reward on completion will be all it takes to accustom him to this new idea.

Once he understands, he will speed up through the tunnel because to him the jump will now represent completion of the task. That's the kind of thinking you want. Next move up to three obstacles by running a sequence of jump, tunnel, jump; reward him big after the last jump. You are on your way!

Once your dog understands the idea, his performance will accelerate as long as you remain cheerful regardless of mistakes. When the dog realizes that the second obstacle, not the first, marks the completion of the task, he will rush to perform it. Soon he will be running through three and four obstacles, then five and six, etc. As you up your ante on the number of obstacles in the sequence, be sure to vary the number of obstacles required before you interrupt to engage the dog in a rousing game with you. If your dog is slowing down, you are upping the ante too quickly for him.

You must work on joy and speed before you add more obstacles. Get out the toys, the treats, the kids—whatever gets him going. Most dogs get revved up over one or the other of the two big motivators—food and fun. You must make running the joyful exercise it can be and you must bring that joy to the agility obstacles. This eager attitude will serve you well, so don't dampen your dog's enthusiasm, no matter what! Remember that your dog's mistakes, and yours, are a necessary part of the process, so embrace them with humor all the way back to the drawing board.

Although you might think you must "correct" your dog's early mistakes, such as going around a jump, I disagree. You would be smart to ignore an accuracy error in favor of speed, and correct your training to solve the problem. I remember, long ago, trying to speed up my Rottweiler Jessy, to whom this book is dedicated, through the weave poles. The first time she tried to rush that stocky

Agility handling includes hand signals and body positioning along with verbal commands.

body, she missed a pole, and my reflexes blurted out the stop command. How sorry I felt. We had been having such fun, and she had been so pleased to be going fast, and the stop rudely burst her bubble. It was a long time before she tried snaking through the poles again; she didn't want to risk it. I learned my lesson! Do you see what I mean? It is better to accept cheerfully the dog's efforts when you are trying to improve speed. Then design another training sequence that sets the dog up to improve his accuracy without error. That's what all of those delightful props are for. You can't always get everything at once, so be prepared to polish a skill here and there separately from your new challenge of sequencing.

Speed up individual obstacles, then combine them to complete two and three in a row, but don't lengthen your dog's sequences until he moves briskly and gleefully through the first obstacle and speeds right on to the second and the third. You have a lot to do with how joyfully your dog approaches each obstacle, so use your imagination and put your energy into every moment of teamwork practice time.

It's important to vary your sequences as soon as the dog is ready so his mind can be kept open to include any obstacles. Agility courses will call for turns away from the obstacle straight ahead, or another obstacle placed near the one that is next. So when teaching your dog to handle obstacles in an ever-lengthening series, incorporate turns, your body language and the names of individual obstacles to help him.

Practice your own timing so you can help your dog before his mind is set on an incorrect route. How independent your dog is and how quickly he moves through the obstacles determine how early you need to command and signal him. The information about what is next should be given before your fast dog is finished with the previous obstacle. Giving the same command only a second later is too late, even though he's not off course yet, for he is already committed to the obstacle he believes is next. It is only fair for you to work as diligently on your handling as you do on his training so that you will become ever more fast, accurate and smooth in your teamwork.

To recap, sequencing brings out your dog's rhythm and helps him think ahead without losing the ability to listen to you and read your body language. Both you and your dog must learn to multi-task in this way, and your ultimate teamwork is an ongoing process. Vary the obstacles in your sequences as soon as you both know what you are doing. The more your dog loves a particular obstacle, the sooner you should include it in a sequence. Use the skills in the following sections to enhance your training and handling as you progress. Celebrate your teamwork!

BACKCHAINING

The principle of backchaining calls for teaching the last item first, then adding the next-to-last item and so on, gradually lengthening the chain of events and always reinforcing and ending with the same final target behavior. This well-studied approach is a wonderful way to break down many complex agility skills. Everything from ramps and contact-zone performance to sequencing and sending skills can be enhanced by the use of backchaining. This process will be referenced in this book as an aid to teaching individual obstacle performance. Backchaining will also be employed as a means to help the dog welcome some less desirable elements of performance, such as staying on the pause table!

As a handler, it is important to remember to continue supporting the dog's path all the way to the target obstacle. That requires more than just your voice or throwing a toy out ahead of the dog. Think of it as an upper body job, leaning forward to encourage forward motion and leaning back to draw your dog back to you. The farther your dog is to go without you, the stronger must be your upper body push toward the target. After you click, you may let down the pressure and throw a toy or run in with a treat, etc. As you backchain the dog's skills, be mindful of backchaining your own handling skills as well.

In the next section, we will use backchaining as an aid to teaching the elements of sending ahead in a simple sequence of jumps.

SENDING AHEAD

Dogs can run faster than humans, so it's to our advantage to be able to send the dog ahead to perform the next obstacle. We can move to our next chosen control point while he is doing his job. This skill is not difficult to train, and it is especially easy if we use a clicker to mark performance of the obstacle.

With an arm signal, the author sends her dog ahead to jump the bar jump.

One very early use of the send skill will be cone games, which are used in the first step of teaching jumping. This is very basic sending, taught by luring just once or twice while clicking at the send/return apex. The dog quickly takes over the job to elicit the click, and then you can gradually add the distance that constitutes a "send" game.

After teaching agility obstacles, we can also use the art of backchaining, as previously described, to make the target obstacle more familiar and therefore more inviting as we increase our distance from it. Here are the beginning steps, using backchaining with only one jump and then adding another.

Prerequisite: Stand beside the jump and invite your dog to jump it. You may face the dog, face the jump or face ahead, as all are useful. You can even do this on leash if your dog is apt to run amok. Click as he jumps, and reward on landing. Do this

The handler runs behind the dog, setting up for the next obstacle as the dog jumps.

with your dog on the right and on the left. This is a good exercise for a Beginner I or Puppy class. On the first repetition, click just for playing the game. After that, greet every effort cheerfully but click only for hind-end clearance of the bar, meaning that the dog is jumping the bar cleanly and not touching it. When the dog is reliable off leash, and when he consistently clears the low jump bar without your moving, begin Step 1 of the "send" exercise (as follows).

Step 1: Stand beside your dog, on either side of but only a couple of feet from the jump, and ask him to jump out ahead of you. You should be able to inspire this step without moving your feet. Click as he lifts his front feet over the jump, and reward with a party on landing. Clicking for front-feet liftoff ensures that you are marking the commitment to the jump rather than perfect execution of the jump. It is only Step 1! Soon we can clean up the jumping, but here we are concentrating on the sending. Next, set up with the dog on the same side as before, one small step farther back. Now send him to the jump, a distance of only a few feet, and click as before. Although these distances are very short, the concept of independent jumping on cue is being instilled. And because we are backchaining the task, the jump itself is becoming a target for the dog because we continue to click as he commits to jump it. The distance is gradually being increased, meaning that the element of sending the dog ahead is being made more difficult.

I recommend practicing Step 1 all on one side in the first session, which would entail several repetitions of each gradually increasing distance. Then, in the second session, I recommend practicing Step 1 with the dog on the other side, following the same progression. The added repetitions of distance work help cement the concept, and both dog and handler end up equally comfortable on either side.

Step 2 of this process adds a second jump before, not after, the target jump. Refresh the target jump with a clicked send, then back up once without the second jump to get adequate distance. Then add the second jump but decrease total distance (following the rule of making one element easier when another is made harder). Step 2 is completed when the dog is comfortable on either side, being sent over two jumps for a total distance of 15 feet. You can see that this is a gradual process and that you have three main variables to manipulate: distance, number of obstacles and relative handler position. It's good to remember to vary, increase and combine your criteria very gradually and also quite often, so as not

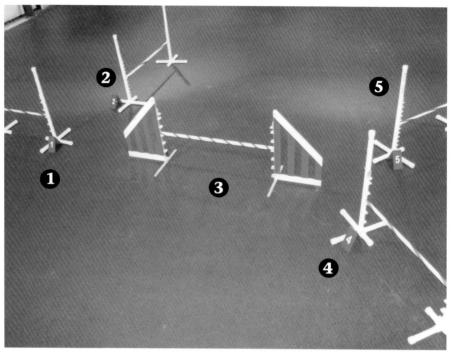

The five-jump configuration used in the sending ahead exercise.

to get stuck at an early phase of the game. The dog needs to remain eager to get to the target jump so that the elements of difficulty can be manipulated without throwing him off.

For a more complex novice example, let's work at sending the dog 12 feet ahead of us to jump the middle jump (jump #2) in in the five-jump configuration shown in the photo above. We know that the dog will happily run along beside us and jump each jump, but here that would constrict our handling choices or slow down the team. So we want to train him to go get the middle jump by himself while we move to the landing side of the third jump (the red winged jump). That skill enables us to execute a front cross (see following section) before he gets to jump number three in preparation for jumping the fourth and fifth jumps with dog on our right side.

FRONT CROSSES AND INSIDE TURNS, REAR CROSSES AND OUTSIDE TURNS

The act of changing sides with the dog while moving through an agility sequence is called a "cross." Agility dogs and agility handlers must have many ambidexterous skills. It is very important to practice with the dog on the left and separately practice the same skill with the dog on the right. But when running a course, it is also necessary to be able to get from one side to the other without causing delay or confusion.

We define a cross to be a "front" cross when the handler crosses the course path ahead of the dog and changes sides with the dog in order to continue smoothly. The dog turns toward the handler, called an "inside turn."

We define a cross to be a "back" or "rear" cross when the handler sends the dog ahead on the course path and crosses behind him. The dog turns away from the handler, called an "outside turn," in order to be on the other side of the handler when the obstacle is completed. Both front and rear crosses are designed to accomplish a change of side in order to preserve the flow of the sequence.

As your training and handling teamwork develops, it is natural to feel a preference for front or rear crosses with your dog. These days we need to have command of both skills, but we are likely to use more of one than the other. Some complex course configurations will lend an advantage to one type of cross over the other, but most changes of side invite the handler to choose either type of cross.

A good example of this openness to interpretation appears in our five-jump example in the last paragraph of the previous section (Sending Ahead). That example has mandated a front cross between jumps number three and four, because that best serves our exercise in sending the dog independently out to jump number two. But if we were not teaching

LEFT: The author sends the dog ahead over a jump. BELOW: As the dog jumps, the author performs a rear cross to change sides.

the dog to send, we have other options, such as a front cross between jumps number two and three or a rear cross between jumps number three and four. In any case, the flow of the sequence is preserved by a change of side.

Front crosses fare very well paired with the ability to send the dog out, as discussed. We will also use front crosses early on in the dog's agility training, such as with the basic cone games we use to teach jumping.

Teaching the dog to send is also important in conjunction with a rear cross. It is not possible to rear cross behind a dog who is behind you. The dog must be willing to pass the handler and continue to the next obstacle before the handler is free to change sides behind the dog.

Some dogs appear to have trouble with rear crosses even though they are willing to go on ahead and perform the next obstacle. They turn the wrong way, as if the handler had not changed sides, appearing not to have noticed the rear cross. Sometimes this is simply a problem of one-sidedness, which is solved by doing twice as many reps to the weaker side. But in my experience this is often a problem with the dog's outside turn training, as it is more natural to turn toward the handler. You should isolate the outside turn training by using your finger pick-up to keep the dog beside you as you perform outside turn circles.

My favorite prop for teaching this concept is one of the large traffic cones like those that you'll use for the cone games. If the dog is on your left, circle the cone to the left and click as his hind end moves toward you. With the dog on your right, circle the cone to the right and click as his hind end moves toward you. Soon he'll be ready to perform rear crosses over a single jump, and you'll be ready to add this fun and useful skill to your handling.

THE THREE Ds: DURATION, DISTANCE AND DISTRACTION

I learned these decades ago in the sport of obedience. The idea is that your dog is not trained until you have added these three complications to each of his tasks. It is very useful to remember these elements of difficulty in our sport as well. Here they are, one at a time:

Duration: How long can your dog stay? Can he hold a contact? Can he wait on the pause table? These are good tests of the dog's ability to "hurry up and wait." We want the dog to be patient, but we also want an explosion of energy the instant we release him. Toward that end, I tend to backchain the elements of difficulty when duration is involved, teaching the release cue before the "don't do anything" cue. This serves me very well.

In the context of obstacle performance skills, I introduce challenges of duration, meaning holding position, before I introduce challenges of distance, simply because we can isolate duration and make it reliable before adding another complication. Any job involving a lead-out necessarily involves duration as well as distance, so teach the element of duration early on.

The challenge in training duration is to keep the dog's enthusiasm high. Using a clicker helps. We lengthen duration by simply delaying the click. We can also use our voices to keep the dog's energy level high as we delay the click, and these happy voice games become important conditioned reinforcers that we can use anytime on the course.

Distance: All of the "send" games you play are a testament to how important it is to be able to handle from a distance, because, as we've said, dogs can run faster than humans. In agility training, it's important that the dog be able to perform his obstacles without our babysitting every detail; the dog's ability to do each job with the handler at a distance is a good test of this. This also serves to remind us that relative handler position is one of the things we need to vary in order to make our dogs self-reliant in their obstacle performance, so be sure to vary the position from which you send your dog to the obstacle. Also remember that distance on individual obstacles comes before distance sequencing.

Distraction: I have had good success with my agility dogs in introducing mild distraction from the outset. This is a very noisy sport, full of ambient activity close to the ring, and I like that. I wouldn't want spectators to be quiet or subdued as they watch a glorious run. I have games for helping beginner dogs ignore the stray food, toys and commotion, and we start such games in my earliest classes.

In general, I follow the rule from clicker-training icon Karen Pryor that we should put our dogs' strongest distractions on cue. I have put on cue not just getting the food or toy, but also sniffing, barking, greeting a friend, diving into the pond, running amok. My philosophy is that, rather than pretend that "nice dogs don't do that," we can control the behavior and while keeping the dog joyous by making deals about just when nice dogs do that.

Once again, the clicker comes through as a perfect marker to signify when the treat is earned. At first that might be on leash, consisting only of one jump or tunnel with a pick-up such that the dog earns the click while facing away from the distraction. Click the finger touch and then immediately front cross and send the dog to the bait bag on the floor. Soon the dog is ready for a bit more. A moderate sequence, for example, might consist of a short doable wait, cue to jump, front cross, pick-up with finger touch (click that touch) and send your dog.

SECTION II

THE OBSTACLES

CHAPTER 6

The Apertures

TEACHING YOURSELF, TEACHING YOUR DOG

Up close, all that agility equipment can look forbidding. Heights seem higher when you picture your dog up there, and a jump looks more imposing when you look around the course and see 12 others just as high, some broader and some just downright strange-

> *He that can have patience, can have what he will.*
>
> —Benjamin Franklin

looking. There isn't much room for error on those planks, and how on earth can a dog be taught to weave so fast through those silly poles?

This section is designed to make agility training logical, fun and seemingly painless. Its goal is to bring you and your dog from introductory work to full competence on the regulation agility obstacles, one by one. If you keep up with the fundamentals and complementary exercises of the earlier chapters, you'll continue to improve your dog's agility quotient.

The regulation obstacles described here are those recognized by the United States Dog Agility Association (USDAA) and the American Kennel Club (AKC). There are other agility organizations worth investigating, some of which use different obstacles or omit some of those included here.

In this section the obstacles are divided into five different chapters based on the different skills required. It's a good idea to become familiar with each chapter before beginning to instruct your dog, but it's not necessary to gain complete competence on one obstacle before introducing another. Just start at the beginning of each chapter and keep track of your dog's progress separately in each area, as he may be quick to learn some skills and slow to learn others. Use this section as a guide, but let your dog dictate the timetable.

Aperture obstacles require the dog to enter a round opening and put his body all the way through in a specified direction. These obstacles include the open tunnel, the closed, or collapsed, tunnel and the tire jump.

OPEN TUNNEL

OPEN TUNNEL INTRODUCTION

The dog must go through an open tunnel, also called a pipe tunnel, of about 24 inches in diameter. Tunnel lengths range from 10 to 20 feet and are generally constructed of coated flexible ducting material.

Most agility dogs love open tunnels and perform them readily. This is a mixed blessing in competition, as it is not uncommon for the dog to prefer the tunnel and enter it even when the handler is trying to direct him to a different obstacle nearby. Advanced competition courses usually include an open tunnel next to the A-frame or dogwalk for this reason. These types of set-ups are called "traps." Choosing the wrong obstacle constitutes an off-course, which results in a fault or elimination.

Your dog can begin tunnel training right away, perhaps with a hula hoop (see Ch. 2) if he is afraid to go through an opening. Hoops, rings and tires are available in various diameters. One that is too big is okay for starters, but too small is not. After a thorough investigation by the dog, the hoop can be tilted over his body and the dog encouraged to walk through, preferably with a treat to his nose in order to minimize stress. Once the hoop presents no threat, introduce a smaller aperture.

Anything from cardboard boxes with the top and bottom open to Styrofoam swim rings can be used to give your dog the concept of putting his body through something. Then it's time for a tunnel.

Regulation-size open tunnels are compressible, so you can start with them short and then stretch them out to lengthen them as your dog gains confidence. Many dogs who start out wary of tunnels are soon charging through regulation tunnels with every bit as much confidence as the dogs who loved them from the first introduction. It depends on the patience and ingenuity of the handler.

Most agility clubs and schools own several regulation-size open tunnels in various lengths and colors. The lightweight and light-colored tunnels are the more inviting. Dogs also should be introduced to heavy and dark-colored tunnels, which tend to make some dogs feel claustrophobic or disoriented.

You should find that the hard part about teaching your dog to go through an opening has already been accomplished before you get to the regulation tunnel. Check some of the backyard ideas in Chapter 2 if your dog is uncertain. In introducing your dog to the real thing, just take it one step at a time and keep his confidence up and the pressure down.

The best motivation for any obstacle is fun! Once the dog learns to love the tunnel, he will race through it with confidence.

OPEN TUNNEL PROGRESSION

STEP 1
- Tunnel is completely compressed.
- Assistant holds dog while you go to other side of tunnel.
- Coax dog through and reward.

Many dogs will be much more willing to go through the tunnel if you stabilize the tunnel on both sides to minimize rolling. Strong elastic stretch cords (bungee cords), passed through the tunnel and hooked together, are good for holding it tightly compressed and keeping the ends wide open.

If your dog is looking at you over the tunnel or tries to go around it, the assistant should touch the dog's nose with a finger and then point into the tunnel. The dog will often follow the finger and then see your face at the other end. "My mom! Who knew?" He should then rush through and greet you effusively. This simple little trick works amazingly well! Another popular trick for helping the dog go through is to have him lie down at the opening rather than stand.

An indecisive dog might go right through on the tail of another dog, so tunnels are great for group work. Often an obedience-trained dog will go through the tunnel at once if his leash is draped through and then you call him, but under no circumstances should a dog be pulled into the tunnel. Some dogs charge right through and some need to stutter-step a bit first. Let your dog work this out. Let the fearful dog watch confident ones go through and get their rewards.

As soon as your dog enjoys the obstacle, give it a name, such as "Tunnel," "Go through" or "Get in." This will become his command to go through any tunnel. Don't introduce your tunnel word while your dog is hesitant.

STEP 2	• Use longer tunnel, 8 to 10 feet in length.
	• Same game plan, just more tunnel between you and dog.
	• Use tunnel word each time.

Increase the length of the tunnel gradually. It doesn't take long to get to full length. At this point you're still enticing with treats and feeding as your dog gets to the exit. It's not wrong to use a clicker on this step, but I do not do so because I'm reaching in with the food, and the food is on the dog's nose before he even gets to the exit. I add the clicker on the next step, when the dog's work is a bit more independent.

Your assistant should let your dog go through as soon as you give your tunnel command, such as "Tunnel" or "Go through." As your dog becomes bolder and pulls toward the mouth of the tunnel, the helper should praise and let him go from slightly farther away. Don't rush this, because some dogs

You may choose to add the clicker at this stage, when the dog is rewarded as he reaches the exit.

who are zeroed in on the aperture are still dependent on the helper's hands and will go around the tunnel if the guidance is suddenly removed. The helper needs to read the dog's intent and give just enough help to ensure that the dog chooses to go into the tunnel.

Some dogs need to remain on leash for this work, but it's nice to work off leash as soon as possible. Then you'll be able to run and play with him as a reward for coming through. Food and other enticements are great motivators, but many of the best agility dogs are also motivated by pure fun, so you may not need treats for every trip through the tunnel.

Even when your dog is delighted with longer tunnels, do a short one now and then to keep his speed and confidence up. Make sure to switch ends, so your dog is comfortable from either direction.

| STEP 3 | • Send dog yourself.
• As you approach tunnel, give dog a signal and tunnel word, then run around to greet him at other end.
• Click clicker as dog's nose exits tunnel. |

It's prudent to shorten the tunnel again for this step. Signal to the aperture with the hand closest to the dog. Hold your treats in the other hand. As soon as you start your dog through, get to the exit with the treat hand. The helper is still stationed at the mouth of the tunnel but should interfere only if your dog tries to avoid entering or turns around inside. Turning around in the tunnel happens often at this step, unless the tunnel is very short, because suddenly the handler's face is not where the dog expects to see it.

If the dog turns around, it's best if the assistant simply blocks the opening when he tries to come back the way he went in while you call your dog from the exit end. Keep your cheerful attitude, motivating success rather than demanding compliance. If your clicking is well timed as the dog's nose exits the tunnel, he'll soon come through fast and straight.

Sometimes you should be on your dog's left side and sometimes on his right when you send him and greet him. He needs to get accustomed to being handled and taking direction from either side.

| STEP 4 | • Gradually extend tunnel to full length.
• Begin by calling dog through as in Step 1, then send dog. |

After your dog is reliable, begin to work without a helper and with the tunnel shortened again at first. Exaggerate your signal at first, pointing directly to the aperture. As the dog gets more and more sure of himself, begin to run several steps past the tunnel exit before rewarding him. If he's not fast, that will help speed him up; if he's very fast, that will help him keep an eye on you.

To keep him fast, remember to send your dog zipping through a short tunnel occasionally even after he's learned to do long ones. This also helps prevent dogs from getting into the habit of turning around in the tunnel. Some dogs even love to spin a few circles in there. Dogs who have time to dance around in the tunnel are not being challenged enough. It happens most often to handlers who are too slow getting to the other end. If that happens, go immediately from the tunnel to another active job, such as an agility obstacle or any other task enjoyable to the whirling dervish. Reward the dog on completion of the subsequent activity. It's easier to

This retriever bursts through the tunnel in anticipation of what's next.

keep your dog's mind on getting out of the other end of the tunnel if he has something exciting to do next.

STEP 5	• Use full-length regulation tunnel. • Send dog. • Gradually introduce tunnel bends. • Add pick-up finger cue with change of direction, and let dog catch you. • Click finger touch and then treat.

From the tunnel entrance, check the amount of daylight coming through. It's not easy to predict what your dog sees with the various bends. You need to let only part of the exit be out of sight at first. It often helps to shorten the tunnel when first bending it. Using a helper and calling your dog through from the other end can also remind him that it's the same job. And of course, the more unsure your dog is, the more gradually you should bend the tunnel.

Once your dog is confident with hairpin turns (which completely eclipse the daylight from the exit hole) in both directions, then start introducing S-curves and extreme shapes. It's great to have a helper again when you first do this, so you can be waiting at the exit and calling your dog to an immediate reward. As his confidence is heightened, resume running past the exit and having him catch up to you.

OPEN TUNNEL SUMMARY

STEP 1: Tunnel is compressed to short length. Assistant holds dog while you go to other side. Coax dog through. Choose tunnel word.

STEP 2: Gradually lengthen tunnel. Use assistant. Use tunnel word. Work up to 10-foot tunnel.

STEP 3: Send dog through shortened tunnel. Use helper to assist if dog turns around. Run to meet dog at tunnel exit. Introduce clicker on this step and click as dog's nose exits tunnel.

STEP 4: Gradually extend tunnel to full length. Using helper, begin by calling dog through just once or twice. Once he's confident, begin sending him yourself.

STEP 5: Introduce bends in tunnel. Use assistant and shorter tunnel length as necessary for very sharp bends. Use your clicker to mark correct exit. Add pick-up and changes of direction at speed as your dog exits, and click the finger touch when he catches up with you.

CLOSED TUNNEL

CLOSED TUNNEL INTRODUCTION

During competitions, the closed tunnel, also called a collapsed or chute tunnel, draws laughter from the crowd. People love to see a dog enter the open end and watch the lump of dog as it runs down the length of chute and pops out the other end.

The dog must enter a rigid opening, approximately 24 inches in diameter and 30 inches in depth, often a barrel with a locking lid ring or a decorative "dog house." Whatever the composition of the open end, the closed tunnel gets its name from a long cylindrical chute of fabric that has been firmly attached to the rigid opening. The chute, which is about 10 feet long and made of rip-stop nylon or pack cloth, is secured to the rigid portion of the tunnel. It lies closed on the ground, and the dog is required to burrow through to the exit.

Problems with the safety of collapsed tunnels are not uncommon. I've had my share of large, rough canine competitors that have hit the fabric hard enough to pull it from the barrel, trapping the dog in a rolling ball of cloth. As you're training your dog for this obstacle, make a game of throwing things over your dog, anything from sheets and blankets to tarps and bags. In the spirit of play

The dog needs to be comfortable with the feeling of the fabric draped on his back.

(and treats!), teach your dog that a sudden brief entrapment is just a game, one that pays very well.

The ring crew at a competition includes a person assigned to straighten the chute after every dog, which minimizes the chances of twisted fabric that could cause entrapment. But life isn't perfect, and someday a chute might snare your dog. You must be ready to step in and get your dog out of trouble if he runs into course problems he can't solve. How to score such an intervention is the judge's problem and depends on case-by-case particulars. When equipment fails, it is ultimately the handler who is responsible for the safety of his dog. The handler should rush in and grab the exit end of the chute and open it wide if the dog gets trapped.

Closed Tunnel Progression

STEP 1
- Chute is folded back on itself to length of 4 to 6 feet.
- Assistant holds dog while you kneel at exit, hold chute open and entice dog through. Reward.
- Gradually drape chute onto dog's back as he comes through, but keep end wide open.

This is treated much like the first step of teaching the open tunnel and, because of that familiarity, progressing through this obstacle should go quickly once your dog accepts the feel of the material on his body. Holding the chute wide open at first is very important.

Your dog should be speeding through the chute and bursting out the exit. This habit is formed early when you begin by showing him the opening at the end and offering an immediate and delicious treat upon his arrival. Stand aside for him when he's charging through! I had a short chute made, which is about 4 feet in length. It makes a wonderful teaching chute in the classroom environment, but the regulation chute, properly managed, can work just fine.

As with the open tunnel, the assistant can start off holding the dog. You should be able to dispense with the leash quickly. An agility leash or tab won't hurt, but the sooner you can work without it, the better. Work on your pick-up exercises in preparation for running with your dog.

STEP 2
- Chute is folded to 6 feet.
- Let middle of chute drape halfway to ground before calling dog.
- Once dog is running through, lower fabric onto his back as he nears exit.

It's time for the dog to begin doing more of the work. Now he has to have a little more faith in himself and be willing to push through to get out. Give him a big cheer as he plows through the section of the chute that has the fabric lowered.

Hold the end open when you first let the chute drop in the middle. Let more of the chute lie closed and gradually drop fabric on the dog as he is running through. Have a big party as he bursts out.

If your dog is not yet running through the tunnel, you need to go back to Step 1 and find a more effective reward system for your dog or he'll get slower as the chute gets longer. Many dogs speed up if you drop the end and run ahead of them just as they get to the exit or throw a ball for them as they emerge. If this step isn't associated with lots of fun, your dog will slow down.

The rewards are for maintaining speed so your dog gets into the habit of whipping through the

The dog should pick up speed in the tunnel and explode through the collapsed side.

material like a dog on a mission. Vary your games and your rewards.

Is it time to name the obstacle? As soon as the dog loves his chute games, you can come up with a command word. Most handlers either say "Chute" or use their open-tunnel command. I recommend using a word different from the open tunnel, and my dogs love to hear the "shhhh" sound of the word chute. When they hear that word, they can find the chute from anywhere and they dive in at full speed.

STEP 3	• Chute is at full length or slightly folded back (8 to 10 feet). • Stand at exit and hold end open. • Call dog and rest fabric on his back as he comes through chute. • Begin dropping more fabric on his back and drop it sooner and sooner until chute rests closed on ground.

Because the closed tunnel is harder to navigate as quickly as the open tunnel, get your dog well motivated for speed before he has to burrow through the long closed chute. While the exit is held open, you can throw his favorite toy or treat for him as his head nears the exit. Throw the reward away from the tunnel to get your dog running through the exit and beyond. Don't throw toys and food into the tunnel. Food in the chute teaches the dog to "vacuum" the chute all the way down. Toys in the tunnels are also likely to slow him down and often leave him in the chute. It is better to fold the chute back to a shorter length and let your assistant throw the toy all the way through, out the end you're holding open. You can also hold the toy yourself and show it to your dog through the open chute, then toss it away as he's emerging. Pretty soon he'll come flying, knowing that you're going to throw the reward.

This shot of the collapsed tunnel clearly shows the rigid opening and where the fabric tunnel attaches to it.

STEP 4	• Chute is folded back to about 6 feet in length and lies closed. • Send dog. • Introduce signal. • Click as dog's nose exits chute. • Add pick-up and click finger touch instead of exit.

As with Step 3 of the open tunnel, run toward the entrance with your dog and get him started yourself. Having mastered the open tunnel already, this should come easily. Remember to work on both your dog's right side and his left side to keep him comfortable with either side. Give an exaggerated signal with your free arm, pointing all the way to the aperture at first. Your assistant needs to be ready to block the entrance if the dog tries to turn back. Your own concern is to get to the exit end fast and greet your dog immediately with his favorite reward as he emerges. When your dog is confident with this, begin to run past the exit a few strides and offer your pick-up, encouraging your dog to catch up with you for his reward. Then make it more interesting by darting a few strides left or right of the tunnel and turning toward him, offering your pick-up with the new hand as he exits. These slight alterations will keep your dog thinking ahead and will make it easy for him to change sides after exiting the chute and moving on to the next obstacle.

STEP 5
• Gradually lengthen chute to full length, sending dog through.

"Gradually" can mean over the course of one lesson for one dog and over a couple of weeks' worth of lessons for another. Don't rush your dog's progress. Cheer your dog on when he pushes through, and reward often. To prepare him for tunneling the entire chute, review Step 3 and practice dropping the fabric on him earlier and more abruptly, then running away from him. Use your pick-up, click the finger touch and have a big party as he gets his treat or chases his toy.

Your assistant's job is very important here. It's not uncommon for a dog that has been charging through a partially draped tunnel to balk or turn around when the whole chute lies on the ground and the handler is at the entrance. It's also natural for the assistant to be taking your dog's reliability for granted by now, so it may come as a surprise if the dog changes his mind. The assistant should block the entrance if the dog turns around, and you should open the exit slightly and invite your dog again, followed by lots of praise as he makes his way through.

Standing to the side of the exit helps your dog get used to not seeing you straight ahead as a target for his tunneling. He may try to take the more direct route to you, so your helper will have to steady him going into the rigid opening.

An arm signal can help the dog decide to go through. Even so, as you taper off on your physical guidance, a snag during this step should not be a big surprise, so don't be alarmed and don't become frustrated. Review the easier steps for a bit if this step seems to be giving you too much trouble, but don't punish your dog. It's quite unlikely that your dog is trying to give you a hard time. Some dogs have a bit of trouble with confidence at this step and need extra time and remedial practice to get it all together.

STEP 6	• Use full-length chute.
	• Run with dog.
	• Introduce angled approaches, wet fabric, wind interference, etc.

When your dog has become very familiar with the closed tunnel, introduce an approach that is not straight-on. The ultimate goal is for him to delight in finding the opening by himself when you call out the chute command. It would be foolish to go from a straight approach to an advanced oblique sendaway all in one step, so break this goal down into gradual steps, angling the approach a little at a time and supporting the effort with your arm signal.

Just as you spend many lessons going from straight to sharply bent with the open tunnel, you need to take a comparable amount of time intro- ducing the dog to an angled entrance to the closed tunnel. You can't bend the rigid opening, so change your start point instead. Start with a clear approach that is farther away than he's used to. As soon as he gets that, introduce angles. Send the dog from slightly off to one side and then the other until he understands how to find the hole for himself from anywhere.

As previously mentioned, sooner or later your dog may get tangled in the chute of a closed tunnel. Yank the exit wide open fast. Don't let him work it out for himself, because his confidence could be damaged badly in a matter of seconds. Quickly show him the way out and give him an active greeting, jumping and playing with him to help him work off the stress of the ordeal.

I find that if the dog gets way off track in the chute, he can't usually right himself again just then. The dog gets used to accomplishing the closed tunnel in a certain way, charging straight ahead, so solutions that require finesse are not likely to occur to him while he is in the chute. First get him out and congratulate his efforts. Just for good measure, your next work should be done with the chute folded shorter and your enticement ready.

Later you may want to set up a tunnel lesson to introduce complications in a controlled way. Wind is a common troublemaker, and it can wreak havoc even with a chute well anchored at the exit. In competition, the judge should position the closed tunnel to minimize conflict with the wind, but it can still be flapping and canted off center as your dog goes through. It's so common to have the closed tunnel affected to some degree by wind that practicing for it should be considered standard preparation for outdoor competitions. Even chutes that are well secured can still flap and make a lot of noise.

When your dog's training in a calm, closed tunnel is complete, and he is delighted to run through without an assistant and from any angle, you are ready to practice for wind. Position the tunnel to be mildly affected at first. To simulate wind problems, begin by having the dog wait at the entrance or having your helper hold him. Hold the exit yourself and flap the chute as your dog comes through. Alternatively, let your helper flap the chute while you send your dog through normally, on the run. You can also anchor your chute off center or pull the top to one side as if the wind had sent it slightly off course.

You should also practice for rain. It's best to introduce that soggy chute without the full rainstorm, so get a bucket of water and dampen the chute a bit. Work up to soaking the chute thoroughly and, of course, actually practicing in the rain! It should be noted that these complications of wind and rain should not be practiced until your dog is brazen through a normal closed tunnel, but these elements can be a lot of fun and add a new dimension to your confident tunneler's ability.

CLOSED TUNNEL SUMMARY

STEP 1: Fold chute back to 4 to 6 feet, or use special short chute. Helper holds dog while you kneel at exit end. Hold chute wide open at first, then less open.

STEP 2: Chute is 6 feet long. Let middle drape halfway to ground before calling dog. Gradually drop fabric on dog's back as he runs through.

STEP 3: Chute is 8–10 feet long. Hold exit open. Call dog through and drop fabric on his back as he comes. Work up to full chute length and drop fabric sooner.

STEP 4: Chute is 6 feet long, lying closed. Send your dog. Play games or throw toy to keep dog running through. Add clicker as nose exits chute.

STEP 5: Use full length of chute lying closed. Send your dog. Play catch-up games and throw toys to keep him running. Add clicker pick-up games.

Tips for Any Obstacle

Use your dog's favorite enticement every time at first to alleviate stress. As the dog becomes more comfortable and proficient with any step in training for any obstacle, use the enticement less often on that step. Always praise your dog's first efforts, and keep training sessions lively and fun.

Use a signal whenever you send your dog. Switch sides with your dog regularly to keep him accustomed to taking commands and signals from either side. With the open tunnel and tire jump, switch ends often as well. Move your obstacles to different locations so that your dog can get used to variations.

STEP 6: Use full length of chute and send dog while running with him. Gradually introduce angled approaches, rain and wind interference.

TIRE JUMP

TIRE JUMP INTRODUCTION

The tire jump, also referred to as the hoop or as simply the tire, is a combination of a go-through and jump. The dog must jump through a tire or ring with an aperture of 18 to 24 inches. The tire is suspended in a frame and secured to the frame on the top and bottom. The bottom of the tire aperture is stationed at the appropriate height for the particular class of dogs. The tire's surrounding frame is constructed of wood, metal or PVC pipe. It is most important that this obstacle be sturdy. The supporting framework must be very strong, with long "feet" to prevent it from tipping if the tire is hit hard from either direction. The rules also specify that the tire must be wrapped securely to prevent a dog from getting a foot caught in a gap. Nowadays most tire jumps are not made with standard tires but with dryer venting hose and reinforced Styrofoam circles.

Most regulations do not specify that the dog must jump through the tire cleanly, and many smaller dogs do use the tire to push off with their hind feet. This actually takes slightly longer than jumping cleanly through and it's not less strain on the dog. Many big dogs have the opposite problem of rapping their feet on the tire when passing through or hitting the top of the aperture with their backs. Add to that the problem, all too common among dogs of all sizes, of passing between the tire and the frame instead of jumping through the hole, and the simple tire jump presents its share of challenges.

TIRE JUMP PROGRESSION

STEP 1
- Tire is touching or nearly touching ground.
- Assistant holds dog.
- You entice dog from other side and reward as he comes through.

An assistant can be useful here, just as in early tunnel training. If your dog needs to be on leash, drape the leash through the aperture before coaxing your dog through. (Do not pull on the leash!) If he's already proficient with leash work, he will see where the leash is and will accept that you want him to follow the leash through the tire. It's the enticement from the other side that makes it seem like a great idea, and your enthusiastic praise as he comes through will tell him he was right. Of course it's also fine to click as the dog comes through, but with the treat already on his nose the clicker is not necessary. I add the clicker as the dog's job becomes his own; that's just my preference.

Let the tire rest on the ground for small dogs and raise it several inches for large dogs. If your dog is uneasy about this new contraption, put your face to the opening from the other side and clap your hands through the hole to encourage him, or let him nibble a treat during his forward progress. The goal is to minimize stress, so don't just order him to come to you and do not name the obstacle until your dog enjoys it.

When your dog loves the tire game, it is time to give it a name and pick a command word. Some people use a tunnel command, such as "Through," for the tire jump, but it's advisable to call it a separate name, like "Tire." The tire jump is easily distinguished on the course, and the dogs quickly learn to pick it out on command. Your dog can learn many individual obstacle names over time, and it's not unusual for a tunnel to be placed near a tire jump, which will be confusing if they are both called "Through."

STEP 2	• Tire is raised 1 or 2 inches higher for small dogs and up to a height of 12 inches for larger dogs. • Assistant holds dog gradually farther away. • You entice dog through and trot backwards as he comes. • Click early, as dog jumps.

During the second step is a good time to add the clicker, as the treat is delayed now. Your helper can line the dog up and point to help him focus through the aperture instead of around it. The faster your dog comes through the tire, the faster you need to run backwards to keep his speed up. Don't make him go slowly! My preference is to click front-end clearance of the tire on this step. I also love to use a retractable leash if the dog is not off leash yet.

You and your dog must have concluded wait training in order to avoid frustration if you have no helper, since you must leave your dog on one side while you go around to the other. I much prefer the command "Wait" rather than "Stay" for this obstacle, since you don't want to inhibit your dog by forcing him to hold still. It's better for him to be at the ready, just holding back in his own chosen position. Whereas "Stay" implies that he may not move a muscle, I train that "Wait" is more forgiving. If I tell my dog to wait while he's in the sit position and he wants to pop up to stand in anticipation, that is fine with me, and it lets the dog take an active part in his own preparation. I want to err on the side of enthusiasm right now.

If you have an assistant, a wonderful variation on this step is to work "around the clock" from the exit side of the tire. The helper keeps the dog perpendicular to the tire on the take-off side while you angle yourself from "12 o'clock" (straight on) to "9 o'clock" on his left and "3 o'clock" on his right. This makes for a dog who knows how to put himself straight to the tire even if his handler is off center on the exit. There are many accidents involving dogs who are not experienced enough with the tire these days, and we can prevent most of those with this sort of early variability training.

An assistant can be worth his weight in treats on this step by preventing early misunderstandings. It's a fine line that the helper must tread, getting the dog focused square to the aperture and holding him back while keeping his forward enthusiasm strong.

> **STEP 3**
> • Raise tire height a bit more for large dogs, to a maximum of 16 inches, and repeat Step 2, running backwards just once or twice.
> • Now begin to send dog through from take-off side and introduce signal.

Your first send-throughs should be done from a standstill in front of the tire rather than running by it. Click as your dog commits to jump through on his own. If he doesn't understand, just put your arm around the tire and hold a treat to the exit side. Entice him through and let him have his reward. Run to meet him as he hops through in order to prevent his coming back to you between the tire and the frame. Start switching sides now, working with your dog on the right as well as on the left. He needs to be "ambidextrous" in agility.

After perfecting this from directly in front of the tire, begin to stand back a little bit so you and your dog can run to the tire. Point to the hole and invite him to go through on his own and click front-end clearance.

As he gets more comfortable with the job, begin to play the catch-up game like you did with the tunnels as a means of delaying the dog's reward and keeping him watchful and fast. The excitement of your running becomes part of the reward, and that's to be encouraged.

Get comfortable with this progression before raising the tire any higher. The bottom of the aperture is only several inches off the ground for the very small dogs and up to 16 inches or so for larger dogs. The exact height should be higher or lower, depending on your dog.

Whether your dog is a jumping machine or a timid jumper, this gradual progression is for helping the dog learn to enjoy going through the hole in the tire and to get used to the many variables he will see while running to the tire obstacle.

STEP 4

- Gradually raise tire to regulation jump height.
- Start dog back farther and run with him.
- Add angled approaches and longer distances between you and dog, and click hind-end clearance.

This step is designed to teach your dog to jump higher, from farther away, at speed and at angles, safely and independently.

Rev your dog up for the excitement of powering through on the run and checking in with you on landing. It's very important to switch sides and to vary other variables, including distance from dog to tire and from handler to dog.

Every repetition needs to be exciting and fun, rewarding and variable. As before, run away when the dog jumps through and reward him when he catches up to you. Also practice changing sides as

Like all jumps, the tire jump is adjusted according to the height class of the dog jumping.

he jumps through so he learns to come out of the tire prepared to change course. It may take weeks to bring your dog this far. Take your time. Don't hesitate to lower the tire while you work on any reliability snags. How quickly you increase the

145

height of the tire depends on how confidently your dog performs the obstacle and how much he likes to jump.

You need to make your dog reliable about being sent through the tire on the run before you reach full regulation height. At each new height, you should teach your dog to take over the job of finding the tire aperture and putting himself through it. Even when your own handler path is different, you should be able to send the dog off at an angle to perform the tire safely and check in on landing. Clicking hind-end clearance of the tire is the best way to help your dog take on this responsibility. Then you meet him with his treat or throw his toy for him.

If your dog hasn't had much experience with different kinds of tire jumps, now is the time to introduce him, at lower heights initially, to all kinds and colors. The tires he meets in competition will vary in size of aperture, size of tire, wrapping

Agility rules specify a minimum diameter of the tire jump, with the intent that dogs of all sizes can fit through.

arrangement and even framework. The more variety he accepts, the better.

I am also a believer in varying the height of the tire jump even after the dog is trained to regulation height. I think he will be a smarter and more resourceful jumper if he is taught to look at the individual tire and jump accordingly rather than launch himself the same way every time. Variations in flooring, terrain, weather, aperture size and individual tire jumps can make for challenging conditions. I want my dogs as smart as possible about sizing up the obstacle for all of these variables. That's the best way to keep them safe at full speed on the course.

TIRE JUMP SUMMARY

STEP 1: Tire is near or touching ground. Assistant holds dog while you go to other side. Coax dog through. Introduce tire command as soon as dog enjoys obstacle.

STEP 2: Raise tire 1 to 2 inches higher for small dogs and up to 12 inches for large dogs. Entice dog through and trot backwards as he comes. Add clicker on this step and introduce "around the clock." Click front-end clearance through tire; that is, click early rather than late.

STEP 3: Raise tire gradually, maximum height of 16 inches. Introduce sending through and running with dog. Click hind-end clearance now rather than front-end; that is, click completion of obstacle rather than commitment to obstacle.

STEP 4: Raise tire gradually to regulation height. Send your dog and introduce angled approaches on the run. Vary distance from handler to dog and from dog to tire. Continue to click hind-end clearance as dog's job becomes more challenging.

CHAPTER 7

The Ramps

We will cover three ramp obstacles: the A-frame, the dogwalk and the seesaw. In addition to requiring the dog to go up and come down via ramps or planks, these obstacles incorporate a safety area at the bottom of each end called a contact zone, into which the dog must step if he is to complete the obstacle without faults.

> The higher your structure is to be, the deeper must be its foundation.
> —St. Augustine

There's nothing different about a contact zone except that it's painted a contrasting color for ease of identification. The zone is required as a safety measure to dissuade handlers from allowing their dogs to leap off the obstacle rather than go all the way down. The cumulative effect of ignoring this safety measure would be injured and worn-down dogs. Agility regulations in all venues enforce the contact zones by imposing performance penalties for missed contacts. With three ramp obstacles on each standard competition course, the faults for ignoring the contacts add up quickly.

CHOOSING CRITERIA FOR CONTACT PERFORMANCE

It's important to think about contact training even when you're working on downscaled or backyard ramp equipment with no painted contacts. After you have fostered your dog's initial delight in being on the ramps for the fun of it, your training techniques should begin to instill in him the habit of running the ramp from end to end and demonstrating your chosen contact criteria on the downside.

Choosing the contact-zone performance criteria for your dog is a matter of deciding two things: first, whether he should stop still or continue to move forward; and second, how he should show you that the behavior is complete.

The most common choices for stopped contacts are: two on, two off (often abbreviated as 2o2o) four on; one on; and four off. These names refer to the dog's feet in relation to the contact zone on the downside of the ramp. Non-stopped contacts can be classified as running or moving.

Many trainers begin teaching contact criteria by clicker-training the dog to touch a simple target with his nose or his paw. That trick can then be transferred to the down-ramp contact zone. This is a great plan, because it's a positive way to focus the dog's attention on a behavior that will incidentally bring him to the desired position. The target can be placed on the downside contact zone itself or on the ground in front of the plank if the desired performance is 2o2o, etc. Of course you must wean from the target as you progress while keeping the position and the behavior you want. This is not a difficult process, but it is precision work to change your click systematically from the target touch to the position of the

The target is placed in such a manner that the dog will receive his reward while in the correct contact-zone position.

front paws. It is a good method, but many trainers are good at shaping the initial target touch and then not so good at weaning from that prop. Don't lose track of your end goal. The target is only a prop being used to make a certain position happen. It is the position behavior that you must eventually reinforce to the hilt, not the target touch.

Whether you decide on target training (or luring), free shaping with the clicker or hands-on guidance, do what it takes to make your dog happy to perform ramp obstacles by running all the way from end to end, including his contact criteria.

He will enjoy this as a win-win game: having fun and receiving rewards while forming correct habits. If you grant contact zone responsibility to your dog too soon, don't blame him for leaping off the ramp. There's a lot going on in his brain. Going all the way up and down the ramp requires some patience, and most dogs, like most people, are in a hurry.

THE OPPOSITION REFLEX

Since you ultimately want a very fast performance, you are well served by encouraging your dog's excitement and speed even while holding the dog back. I know this sounds like bad advice, but this has been well shown to foster a forward-thinking performance by activating the dog's opposition reflex in the right direction. As he wants to go faster, he will lower his center of gravity and pull you, bringing his center of gravity forward. This is exactly the position you'll want at breakneck speed when he's fully trained. Therefore, even at this fundamental level you want to invite that behavior and that thinking. So remember to praise him even as you are holding his collar. You will be helping him learn to balance and drive with power all the

Introducing your dog to the A-frame may entail leading him over it and offering treats as he walks; let your dog's personality set the pace.

way to the end. This is the same psychology used to teach sled dogs the proper pulling technique. This lowering of the center of gravity at speed will also help your dog hit a difficult weave pole entry someday, but it is especially important in keeping the dog secure at speed when he's up in the air on the ramps. The dog will be faster, safer and more efficient if he drives with his center of gravity lowered and forward. You will find a lot of opportunity for this artful use of opposition reflex training in your agility dog, everything from tunnels, jumps and start lines to weave poles and contacts. It will be lots of fun to start your ramp training with this in mind.

The sport of agility rewards speed, to be sure, but only if accuracy is not lost. So don't dampen your dog's forward thinking. Develop in him the drive to run forward with power and glee. Along the way, develop the ramp and contact-zone habits that will keep him safe and accurate.

A-FRAME

A-FRAME INTRODUCTION

The A-frame is constructed of two sides, each 3 feet wide and 9 feet long. The dog must scale this obstacle by going up one side and down the other, touching the painted contact zone at the bottom.

For stability, the A-frame is braced underneath. The hinged ramps are secured to each other near the bottom with metal or wood. Chain is a popular brace material for adjustable A-frames. The ramp surfaces are specially prepared for good traction.

Even a young pup can begin A-frame training right away, and you don't need a regulation obstacle for the first try. A basic incline can be fashioned at home by leaning ramps on steps. It's helpful to practice first inclines with your dog in a casual way to keep it fresh and fun.

A regulation A-frame that is adjustable is great for learning. Training on the A-frame is also greatly enhanced by group work. The more confident dogs are invited to go across first and are praised wildly as they succeed. That makes it much easier for others to follow and learn how it's done. The wide ramp is very inviting, and whole litters of pups cavorting on very low A-frames are well documented in agility homes.

A-FRAME PROGRESSION

STEP 1
- A-frame has apex height of about 3 feet.
- Let dog check it out and climb to the tune of praise and treats.

The first task is not so much to get the dog over the obstacle as to make him comfortable with it. That's why even a one-sided backyard ramp will do as a first introduction. The clicker is welcome on this step, but it is not necessary. With the food and toys coming continually, clean clicking can get pretty tricky, so there's nothing wrong with adding the clicker on the next step when the dog will do more operating. To use the clicker correctly on this step, capture the act of the dog's moving forward up the ramp and then quickly move the reward to the dog. It is all too easy to capture accidentally the dog's behavior of stopping or looking at you rather than at the obstacle, etc. It would be better to reward your dog continually and just play with him while he gets used to the obstacle if you feel you might click incorrectly.

Rushing up and over the A-frame is not the best initial strategy for every dog, so allow your dog to be himself. If you feel his confidence would be enhanced by your use of enticements to lead him over the obstacle, or allowing him to follow another dog, then by all means do so! Even turning around on the ramp is fine by way of exploration and confidence-building on his first introduction. This need not be treated as a regulation obstacle yet, so you also should not name the obstacle at this point.

The dog's confidence will tell you how much luring and reinforcement to use, and his personality will tell you how active and silly he needs you to be. Have your enticement ready and always congratulate your dog's first efforts.

In addition to food and toys, effective enticements for reluctant dogs may include the following: walking on the A-frame with your dog; sitting on the A-frame with your dog and petting him while he relaxes, then walking him off; having a second person hold him while you come to the apex from the other side, then calling him to you; and playing on the A-frame with a trained dog while your dog watches. Use anything to help your dog relax and anticipate pleasure while on the A-frame. One note of caution: the lower the apex of your A-frame, the more force the hinges must bear. Support the middle or put an upended cinder block under each board near the apex.

Don't name the obstacle until your dog enjoys it and is running it from end to end. As with the aperture obstacles, practice from the beginning with the dog on your right side as well as on your left side.

Dogs that lack confidence often tend to get too close to their handlers while on ramps, and this becomes precarious as the ramps get steeper. Through the artful use of treats it is easy to teach your dog to work in the middle of the ramp rather than hug either edge. Whenever you reach in to give a treat, present the treat in the middle of the ramp even if your dog is hugging your side. Move the treat right past him and put it in the middle. If the treats always happen in the middle, he will learn to pay attention to the middle as well, and eventually he will be strong enough to keep his body there.

Delivery of the treat in the middle of the ramp regardless of the dog's position is important in order in order to change a dog's habit of staying close to the edge.

STEP 2
- Apex is raised to about 4 feet.
- Raise only when dog is ready.
- Add contact position (see Choosing Criteria) and clicker.

Remember, *fast* does not necessarily mean *confident*. Some dogs want to run across the obstacle in order to get away from it. In that case you need to keep the A-frame lower and spend more time building confidence with a high level of reinforcement. A confident dog is pleased to be on the obstacle and will happily interact with you on the incline, going up or down.

With super-fast dogs I like to make a game of running and pausing, because it improves the dog's balance and his command over his body at speed. It doesn't take a lot of repetitions, just enough to ensure that he is not a victim of his own inertia. In order to stop he must lower and shift his center of gravity, as discussed in the section on opposition reflex. This will make him more secure as you give him more responsibility at speed. Now rev him up and go!

The A-frame should still be low enough to present no physical difficulty for him. It's better to raise it no more than a foot to make sure your dog gets a feel for the obstacle and builds his strength and accuracy along with his confidence. That will make it easier for him to climb properly when the A-frame is steeper. You should begin to delay the reward until he's well into the downside contact zone. Don't delay the treat until he's off the obstacle just yet, because it's being in the contact zone that you're trying to reward just now. Remember that these are your fundamentals and you will need this good habit as you give your dog more responsibility. Whatever your chosen contact performance criteria, the dog needs to believe that the area at the bottom of the ramp will pay very well.

Once you've chosen the best contact-zone performance criteria for this dog, begin to guide him into that position on all sorts of ramps. Most trainers do not begin this contact training on the regulation A-frame itself. It's better to teach the behavior on other inclines and then transfer the well-learned trick to the contact obstacles. And, as with any other trick, you'd do well to teach the behavior by shaping it with a clicker. You will need this position to be happily and freely offered by the dog rather than commanded by you. His contact position must become a well-loved and trusted friend to both of you!

STEP 3
- Gradually raise A-frame higher.
- Continue to bolster dog's enthusiasm and accuracy.
- When dog is reliably offering correct contact performance, begin to add complexity for independent contact work at speed.

Most dogs are not fully reliable about their contact criteria at this point. I don't see a problem with this as long as you continue to progress toward that reliability. If you are still luring the dog into his final position, you need to start weaning the dog from your intervention. Are you still helping him remember to touch a target? Is he running down the ramp toward your lowered hand? Does he stop short of the contact and need you to tell him to take another step? Does he put one foot on the ground and need you to remind him to place the second foot? These are just a few examples of behaviors that need cleaning up. Your clicker is the best tool for this. If it's a target touch or position, such as sit or down, that needs work, then practice elsewhere until the dog is offering the desired behavior, and then bring that trick to the lowered A-frame. Click the desired behavior and then bring out the reward. It's very important to keep your clicking clean if you want the dog to look at the ramp rather than at you.

As you make the A-frame steeper, your dog needs to lean forward and use his hindquarters more forcefully. If the obstacle is raised gradually, your dog will take this all in stride. If you rush the raising of the A-frame, your dog will either slip back or fear that he might fall. That unsteady feeling comes from not using his rear muscles properly for propulsion. Once he has that feeling of falling back, he will compensate by either balking at the obstacle or by jumping onto it.

Many dogs develop the habit of jumping onto the obstacle in order to feel secure about getting to the top. A dog may look brave when he's leaping on like that, but it can reflect insecurity about scaling the height, so assess what's going on for your dog. It might be wise to spend extra time with the apex just high enough to require significant propulsion from the rear. Use an enticement to start him from a standstill close to the ramp, and use the leash or collar to make his first step onto the obstacle a short step. Use your clicker to mark that first footfall onto the ramp and follow that with the reward. This first step will not ultimately be a slow step, just a shortened stride. Now the dog must power from the rear to ascend the ramp from there. A strong healthy dog should be happy to use his hindquarter muscles to propel him up, and this is a faster way to scale any ramp.

Now what about the sighthounds and other powerhouse jumping dogs? Dogs that leap like gazelles likewise have to be taught to make the first

Once a dog has gained confidence and enjoys the A-frame, it's up and over with ease.

step onto the contact obstacle a short step. If the dog likes food, it's a simple matter to put a few well-placed tidbits in the contact zone and up the A-frame or to hold his agility collar with one hand and an enticement down low with the other. Some jump-happy dogs just plain love to jump onto anything. They are not necessarily crazy until they have the opportunity to fly through the air. Superdog sees the A-frame as just another tall building to leap in a single bound. Some of these dogs, notably the sighthounds, can literally jump to the apex from the ground. These wonderful jumpers can rack up 30 or 40 faults per course on contact zones alone without lacking a speck of confidence.

It is not enough just to teach these dogs to trot onto the A-frame. Their trotting strides are so strong that they often put their first foot above the zone and hop their back feet past it. They are not being stubborn and they are not afraid of the steepness. It's their natural way. They are so spring-loaded and well-coordinated that they bounce from the ground to the apex without even thinking about it, so walking them onto the equipment is sometimes not enough. Even with your hand in the agility collar, some of these dogs can miss the zone.

If the dog is also sensitive, as is often the case, and you lose your patience or come down with a heavy correction, the dog is apt to respond with indecision or by balking at the A-frame, a result of worrying about the correction he anticipates. That probably means he does not understand your criteria. You are fighting nature here, and you would be smart to use a positive approach if you'd like to keep the dog working with you.

Something the dog finds hard to resist (like a white plastic bag if he's a lure courser or a cloth with animal scent on it if he's a hunter) can be used to get his mind off the apex and focus him down where you need him. Any trick that makes your dog happy to work well in the contact zone is fine. Using one person on either side, each with a guiding hand in his collar or on a tab, can help him get the idea. Praise lavishly when he takes the mincing first steps you want him to take.

It's important to keep the A-frame at the dog's transition height for a long time so he will develop proper skills and habits. Make sure the dog is happy to take a small first step onto the obstacle, placing his foot on the first or second cleat up, before you raise the A-frame slightly higher.

It's hard to make yourself work slowly with the A-frame when you know that your dog can practically leap over the whole thing end to end already, but then that's the problem. You will pay later in accuracy much more than it will cost you now in time and pride to work conservatively.

> **STEP 4**
> • Gradually raise A-frame to full height.
> • Further improve control for contact zones by varying the "Three Ds."

When your dog is demonstrating independent performance with the A-frame and with his contact criteria, it's time to add the "Three D" elements of distractions, distance and duration. Of course, these complications are varied one at a time and each needs to be presented to the dog as a win-win game.

With correct contact-zone position, the dog looks to his handler for approval.

Your dog is already familiar with the simple distractions of life as he goes about his agility training, but here we are talking about the big D of handler distraction. This means that you have trained his A-frame and contact performance to be so independent that you can cross behind or in front of him while he is performing, you can run quickly or slowly, you can come up behind him or you can pass him and be out in front, and he still knows to run the obstacle and perform his contact behavior just the same. You have already been working the variable of distraction. Here it is just more challenging, and every dog will have different weaknesses in this department. Most dogs find it difficult to "let the handler run away," so this big D deserves some concentrated attention.

The big D of handler distance includes the obvious challenge of sending the dog to the A-frame while you move parallel to him some distance away. Distance work is even more important when the handler starts close by and must veer away on the run while the dog is on the obstacle. This is much more advanced and must be taught systematically, just as you shaped the dog's independence from handler position in Steps 2 and 3. Begin with a 45-degree angle and a steady pace, praising the dog and clicking immediately as he completes his contact requirement. In other words, do not combine the big Ds of distance and duration until you have taught the dog about each variable separately.

The big D of duration comes into play whenever the dog completes his contact behavior before the handler wants him to tackle the next job. The dog is not allowed to charge ahead blindly to perform whatever is in front of him. He must hold himself until the handler indicates the next assignment.

It is up to you whether you train your dog to wait automatically on every contact or you want him always to continue straight ahead unless you tell him to wait or to turn. There are advantages and disadvantages to each method. Generally, the slower handlers tend to expect their dogs to wait, which is taught at this step simply by delaying the click after the dog assumes his required position. If you praise the dog as you delay the click, he will understand that you are not expressing dissatisfaction with his performance by withholding the click.

In short, during your practices you need to train your dog to perform all of the contacts properly, no matter what. Good habits are formed at home, so pay extra attention to your contact training on every ramp obstacle. Contact training is never a finished product!

A-FRAME SUMMARY

STEP 1: Apex is about 3 feet high. Let dog check it out thoroughly and enjoy learning about his balance on the obstacle. Initial clambering all over helps balance.

STEP 2: Raise apex to about 4 feet when dog is ready. Run the ramps from end to end. Use clicker to introduce contact zone criteria.

STEP 3: Gradually raise apex higher. Continue to improve contact performance, using clicker to help dog take responsibility.

STEP 4: Gradually raise apex to full height. Further improve control training by maintaining criteria while complicating your variables. Use and perfect the Three Ds.

DOGWALK

DOGWALK INTRODUCTION

The dogwalk, also known as the balance beam, is made up of three narrow planks and two raised supports. The dog must go up one plank in a specified direction, traverse the raised plank at a height of about 4 feet and descend the third plank on the other side. There is a contact zone at the bottom of the two end planks for safety's sake, as discussed.

Each of the 3 planks is about 12 feet long and 12 inches wide. Two of the planks are end ramps, each secured to a tall support on one end and resting on the ground on the other end. Like the A-frame ramps, the dogwalk planks are specially prepared for good traction.

It is not easy to predict what an untrained dog will do, and you don't want to find out when he's balancing on a narrow plank 4 feet in the air. Downscaled dogwalks should be practiced before introducing the regulation walk. Some regulation dogwalks are adjustable, which is a great feature for newcomers. Many fine professional models of "baby dogwalks" are also available, most with 8-foot planks rather than 12-foot planks. We've also discussed some of the things you may have in your own backyard that can be used to introduce various agility obstacles (see Section I).

DOGWALK PROGRESSION

STEP 1

• Start with ladders laid flat on ground and planks on low blocks.
• Confidence, balance and coordination.

You can lure shamelessly and cajole your dog to follow through or use your clicker to capture the dog's behavior of putting his feet on the plank or between the ladder rungs. Either way, you should be active and inspiring so you can up the ante quickly. Your dog should soon be moving forward with all four feet in play on these makeshift obstacles. Perhaps you have already had some fun clicker training your dog to trot through the rungs of a ladder, as mentioned in Chapter 2. This is terrific preparation for dogwalk work! And have you taught your dog to back up? This is another great proprioceptic skill for the dogwalk.

As you work through the steps of dogwalk training here, you might also consider clicker training your dog to back up in the rungs of the ladder, combining the two prerequisite skills. It might seem unrelated to dogwalk work, but these kinds of skills will make your dog much more self-aware, balanced and coordinated as he begins to run the regulation 36-foot length of this obstacle. The smarter you can make him about where all his feet are in space, the safer you make him as he tears across at full height and full speed.

The first planks you use should be about 12 inches wide and set on cinder blocks or any low support. Most dogs have no aversion to trotting along a raised single plank. If your dog doesn't like the narrow plank, start with two planks next to each other and gradually separate them. At first the dog will use the whole

The ladder exercise teaches a dog to be aware of his footing and coordination.

width of the two planks, but as the gap between them gets wider, he chooses one or the other.

Let the plank wobble only after your dog loves it. When your dog is really confident, use a hand or foot to make the board bounce while you play, click and treat.

Some dogs need more practice being off the ground than others, and many larger dogs dislike the bounce of the board. The weight of your dog, the bounce in his stride, the length and thickness of your plank and the distance between supports will all contribute to the spring in the board as your dog explores the plank.

STEP 2
- Downscaled dogwalk, about 2 feet high.
- When the dog loves this obstacle, introduce contact criteria, using clicker and reinforcing every correct repetition.

It bears mentioning that leaping onto the plank with all fours is one of the happier dogwalk problems to face. It should not be corrected. Rather, make a mental note to issue more guidance next time, even perhaps using the agility collar and enticements to help the dog focus down low at the ends of the planks. This will slow the dog down for a repetition or two but will keep his confidence high and his attitude positive. His speed will return very easily and he'll be better able to handle it.

It also bears mentioning that some dogs display sudden insecurity at this step. Of course there are many ways to help. My favorite interventions use the 24-inch pause table. I want to begin by letting the hesitant dog get off the ramp instead of getting on. Place the pause table beside one ramp, just above the contact. The dog hops onto the table, steps onto the ramp and walks down to the ground to the tune of wild praise and rewards. This approach helps dogs feel in control and capable. After a couple of

A way to help a hesitant dog is to let him step onto the middle of the ramp from a pause table so that he only has to walk part of the way down.

repetitions, go the other way and have the dog climb the ramp and step onto the table.

Because the table is as high as the traverse ramp, you can gradually move it back toward the middle of the obstacle, at which point the dog is stepping onto the traverse ramp from the table and then running half of the dogwalk, one way or the other, to the ground. At each position, also have the dog run from the ground to the table. The clicker marks the behavior of moving forward on the plank. The ante is raised until all delivery of rewards happens on the planks as well, and the table affords relief but no clicks and no goodies.

I'm sure you get the picture. Very quickly, the same dogs that were reluctant to perform the downscaled dogwalk from end to end are now running merrily up and down the ramps to the pause table. Less and less time is spent on the table until they just don't need it any more, and they run right by it to the reward on the ramp instead.

STEP 3

- Adjustable regulation dogwalk with the traverse ramp set unevenly, one end 2 feet high and the other end 3 feet high.
- Vary heights at both ends.
- Work low to high, then high to low.
- Help dog take responsibility for contact criteria at speed.

This Doberman Pinscher crosses a regulation dogwalk in competition.

Even though it might seem that the dog's head should be up, that's not the case. The expert dogs carry their heads low to pay attention to the obstacle and their next steps. Using enticement such as treats is fine, but keep your dog low to help him focus down and ahead on the plank.

It is good to prop the planks from underneath as necessary to minimize bouncing for awhile. You should reintroduce the bounce later, just as you did in Step 1.

As the dog's ability improves, use your clicker to introduce your contact criteria just as you did on the A-frame. Reward your dog every time for contact performance; don't assume that you can pick up where you left off in your A-frame proficiency.

Your encouragement is still important, and there's nothing wrong with giving your dog a treat while he's running the plank. It's good to learn to "walk and chew gum at the same time," but if he needs to stop to eat, that's okay for now. I'm also fond of clicking the forward running of my toy-loving dogs and then giving them a toy to carry the rest of the way.

It's time to employ the many devices and tricks that help the dog cement the habit of hitting the contact zones (see A-frame). By the time you are ready for Step 4, your dog should be clicked and treated only in the contact zones, so he should be running as fast as he can to get there!

STEP 4
- Regulation dogwalk.
- Introduce independent contact work at speed and perfect Three Ds (distance, distraction and duration).

As your dog becomes proficient at the regulation dogwalk, further his education by getting him accustomed to more unsteadiness in the planks. Many older dogwalks have started to bow and sag, creating some bounce at speed. If your own dogwalk is sturdy, you need to make sure your dog still enjoys a bounce and can balance on an inclined ramp when it bounces. Make your dog a real expert, ready for any dogwalk. A bouncy dogwalk should pay off very well!

As you give your dog more freedom of choice on the dogwalk, remember to put effort into the systematic training of the Three Ds. They will not automatically transfer from the A-frame work you have done.

DOGWALK SUMMARY

STEP 1: Twelve-inch-wide plank set up about 12 inches off ground and aluminum extension ladder, compressed and laid flat. Play clicker games and reward dog while he's on plank and in ladder. Advanced dogs can also back up.

STEP 2: Downscaled dogwalk about 2 feet high. Introduce contact performance when dog is happy and confident from end to end.

STEP 3: Adjustable regulation dogwalk, setting one end to 2 feet and other to maximum of 3 feet. Vary heights and run low to high, then high to low. Help dog take responsibility for contact criteria at speed.

STEP 4: Regulation dogwalk. Reward contact performance. Continue to vary variables and incorporate training for Three Ds: distance, distraction and duration.

SEESAW

SEESAW INTRODUCTION

One of the favorite obstacles of spectators, the seesaw or teeter, cements the image of an agility course as a big playground. The dog needs an extra measure of balance and patience to do well on this obstacle. He must go up an inclined plank that is 12 feet long, which is secured to a fulcrum about 2 feet

The tippy plank introduces the variables of the seesaw on a shorter board and at a lower height.

high. The dog must tip the raised end and bring it to the ground, then dismount. The dog must touch contact zones both ascending and descending. The seesaw is slightly weighted on one end or attached an inch or so off center so it will return itself to the proper position for use from the same direction over and over.

From a dog's eye view, this obstacle looks much like the dogwalk from the end—a 12-inch-wide inclined board with a contact zone. But halfway up, what a surprise as the plank starts to tip! This sudden instability is dreadfully rude and, if not introduced gradually, can create a lasting distrust of this obstacle. It should be introduced after your dog is secure with the fundamentals (Ch. 2) and is well balanced and confident on narrow, bouncy planks (see Dogwalk, Step 1).

The seesaw presents three major elements of difficulty: noise, balance and height. This training is designed to separate these elements and build a huge bank account of skill and confidence in each. The element of noise is tackled first, because it is such a common source of concern among dogs. Agility is a noisy sport, and the seesaw is an especially noisy obstacle. The element of balance is next, because the seesaw requires more comprehensive balancing skills than the other ramp obstacles. Then the familiar element of height is added last by way of complicating the dog's command of the other two skills.

The seesaw is likely also to challenge you as a trainer. Can you shape each of these elements of difficulty beyond your dog's mere tolerance of what the obstacle will do when he mounts it? Top competition dogs can easily complete the seesaw in 1.5 seconds. They don't tolerate the obstacle; they love it!

SEESAW PROGRESSION

STEP 1
- Introduce tippy plank and wobble board.
- Use clicker to shape investigative and playful behaviors.
- Reward noise, then balance.

A downscaled seesaw, or tippy plank, is well worth buying or building. Many companies offer these low-fulcrum 8-foot planks with adjustable bases. The purpose of the tippy plank is to introduce the elements of difficulty associated with seesaw performance, but at low heights.

On the first introduction, I prefer to invite the dog to investigate the high end of the plank, which is only several inches off the floor. As for the process of shaping for noise, the goal is to click as the plank hits the floor. But if your dog is fearful, it's your call whether to click for touching the plank, and then for moving the plank and then for hitting the floor with the plank. Your dog will let you know his confidence level by his body posture, most notably whether he is leaning forward or back as he sniffs the new toy!

Remember that shaping for noise with the plank is different from requiring the dog to get onto the plank. Don't up the ante by requiring the dog to get on until he is happily getting "rich" in rewards by slamming the raised end to the floor. Time your click to that noise. This is the initial deposit into the bank account of confidence for the element of noise.

For a backyard version of a tippy plank, just prop an 8-inch plank onto a scrap piece of 2 x 4 lumber and then change the fulcrum as your dog's confidence improves. The unsecured fulcrum has the advantage (and perhaps the initial disadvantage) of shifting as the dog begins to operate forcefully on the plank. This will improve his balance more, as does the wobble board.

A wobble board is a platform with a rounded fulcrum under the middle, so it tips in every direction. As with the tippy plank, the first clickable event with this contraption is making noise. After the dog is demanding that you click and pay him for slamming the thing around, then up the ante to

The wobble board accustoms the dog to balancing himself on a moving object as well as to the noise of the board hitting the ground.

require two paws on, etc. Soon he will be riding the unstable platform, and you will be clicking and paying for his balancing efforts. You can complicate his job by using your foot to rock the platform. This toy is wonderful for working all the side support structures of the dog's spine as he shifts his weight constantly for balance.

These games should be played with lots of laughing and fun. Continue to love the noise as you play harder! You'll be building a big account of skills and confidence.

STEP 2
- Adjustable regulation seesaw, fulcrum at 8 to 12 inches.
- Work high to low, then low to high.
- Raise fulcrum gradually.
- Introduce contact criteria with guidance.
- Name obstacle only if dog is ready.

As with the dogwalk, a regulation seesaw that is adjustable is a wonderful training obstacle. This has a full-length plank, which will operate less abruptly than the 8-foot plank used in Step 1, but the raised end of this plank will be higher.

Begin at the high end, about 16 inches high, and use your hand to bring that end halfway to the ground. Play with your dog just as you did in Step 1, cheerfully inspiring him to make noise with the plank. Click the noise as before. Just one or two repetitions of this game is all it takes. Then go to the low end and shape the behavior of running the whole plank from end to end.

So many dogs have trouble with the seesaw that it deserves extra time and patience. These downscaled seesaw games help the dog understand the concept of the obstacle. Your dog learns to welcome and control the strange sudden motion. This is very different from simply tolerating the motion! He needs to own it and enjoy it.

As with all obstacles, don't name the seesaw until your dog is comfortable with it. If you use the seesaw command while your dog is afraid of the motion, the word will conjure up images of insecurity. You will need to name the seesaw by Step 4, when all elements of difficulty are in place.

For sensitive dogs, you can spot the plank to make it tip smoothly at first. For many dogs, a spotter represents the ounce of prevention that is worth a pound of cure. If your dog needs to operate thoughtfully and carefully, let him do that, and his speed will come after his confidence. The brazen dogs can operate either with or without a spotter, because they have enough confidence in their bank accounts to cover any minor incident that may occur.

In order to shape the behavior of running forward on the plank, remember to click the posture you want. That sounds obvious, but it's easy to make the mistake of clicking when the dog looks at you or hesitates. You want instead to capture him with his center of gravity forward, facing ahead and working the plank. Touching the contact zone at the end might still require your help at this stage and also might warrant a separate click.

Go on to the next step when your dog is running the 12-inch fulcrum seesaw happily for a single click, working all the way to his contact position and nailing his criteria there with a "Ta da!" expression on his face.

STEP 3	• Introduce element of height using seesaw table games. • Game 1: regulation seesaw at full height with 24-inch pause table under high end. • Game 2: two pause tables of different heights.

Begin on the table and work first from high to low. You should initially lower the plank halfway as in Step 2. You lower the plank halfway to the table, and the dog lowers it the rest of the way—slam! He's playing the game and he loves to make noise. Then work low to high, from ground to table. No spotter for the plank now! Your dog needs to welcome the tipping of the plank and make as much noise as he can make. These games help him learn to feel the pivot point and automatically lower his center of gravity without feeling the need to stop.

In the two-table game, the dog runs from platform to platform without hesitating. Invite a few repetitions of this game as needed for increasing speed and confidence but not for contact work. These seesaw table games are for isolating the third element of difficulty, height. We will be putting it all together soon enough.

ABOVE: Using the pause table helps the dog get used to the pivot point without the plank's fully lowering. BELOW: Getting onto the seesaw from the pause table, the dog lowers the plank as he steps on, thus getting accustomed to the noise.

Go on to the next step when your dog is completely relaxed and fast with the seesaw games of Steps 2 and 3. It is through these games that he cements his skills and confidence with the elements of noise, balance and height. He should run up, down and across without hesitation. He should keep his balance smoothly and in harmony with the plank as it tilts.

STEP 4	• Regulation seesaw, full height.
	• Name the obstacle.
	• Dog gradually takes responsibility for contact position.

Hold your dog's collar and show him the seesaw. Tip the plank to show him that it moves. Let him investigate, and incorporate opposition reflex work as discussed earlier in the chapter. This helps your dog realize in a relaxed way that this is the same obstacle he played with on the tables, but the landing platforms are now gone.

Agility lends itself well to a positive application of mimicry. It does help a new physical challenge go more smoothly if your dog can watch it being done correctly and associate that with pleasure. If you can let an accomplished dog take a few regulation seesaw turns while your student dog watches from the side, it will be very helpful in building your dog's desire to have his own turn to work his friend, the seesaw, especially if you're the one rewarding the demo dog!

You wouldn't be on this step if your dog didn't have the three elements of difficulty mastered, so it's time to name the obstacle if you haven't done so already. The seesaw should have a command different from that used for any other contact obstacle. Even if you prefer to use a single "Walk it" command for the A-frame and dogwalk, the seesaw should be called something different to alert the dog

Border Collie Emmy Lou handles the seesaw in a NADAC trial.

to the obstacle that rocks. He should not have to guess if the plank he is ascending will start to move.

Bring back your contact work, at first with your guidance and then following the same steps you used to transfer that responsibility to your dog in the A-frame work.

STEP 5
- Full contact responsibility and vary your variables
- Introduce the Three Ds of distance, distraction and duration.

Gradually decrease your influence until your dog is taking full responsibility for sticking the contact correctly, from both ahead of you and behind you, while you cross in front and when you invite him over the obstacle from the high end rather than run with him. The regulation seesaw is a complicated yet short-duration obstacle, so he needs to own this performance completely.

Sometimes problems with the contact zones develop only after the dog has become very familiar with and enamored of the obstacle. So while your dog is still performing correctly on the seesaw contacts, take steps to keep him that way. Continue to use your clicker on brilliant seesaw performances.

One note regarding the extreme shaping that you have done to build confidence on the seesaw: though it's tempting to click some wild antics that you welcomed on the tippy plank earlier, do not carry those games over to the regulation-height seesaw or you will make your dog very sloppy as well as very brave. The "kamikaze" dogs can scare you to death jumping onto the high end of the plank or twirling around on the regulation plank as it's falling. Ignore your dog's efforts to get your attention through recklessness now that the element of height is part of the picture. Be proud of his confidence and don't dampen his enthusiasm, but make his job more challenging by varying your variables and upping the ante with the Three Ds, just as you incorporated these challenges into your A-frame work.

SEESAW SUMMARY

STEP 1: Tippy planks and wobble boards. Use clicker and reward noise, then balance.

STEP 2: Downscaled seesaw with regulation plank. Use spotter to control plank if necessary. Reward noise, then balance. Add basic contact control with your guidance. Name obstacle only if dog is ready.

STEP 3: Seesaw table games, using one table and then two tables of different heights.

STEP 4: Regulation seesaw without props. Dog takes independent control of obstacle. Dog takes responsibility for contact criteria.

STEP 5: All elements of difficulty in place, perfect performance while varying Three Ds of distance, distraction and duration.

CHAPTER 8

The Jumps

Jumping may be the single most important skill required in the sport of agility. Good books have been written on the subject of jumping. One that details a program specifically designed for agility is *Jumping From A to Z* by Christine Zink DVM, PhD and Julie Daniels, published by Canine Sports Productions.

> *"I can run that course in 25 obstacles! Just watch her face at number 18..."*
> —Superman, the ultimate wild child Border Collie

You will see several types of jumps on an agility course, and they come in many different sizes, shapes and colors. Most agility jumps have stanchions of wood, metal or PVC pipe on either side. Some jumps have "wings," referring to decorative frameworks that extend a few feet out from either side of the jump bars. Jumps may have one or more jump bars in place, with the top bar positioned at the official jump height of the class. The top bar of an agility jump is required to be displaceable. This helps prevent injuries and also indicates in competition whether the dog's performance should be faulted.

Jump height categories are determined by the height of the dog at the withers (top of the shoulder blades). The dog may be entered in a higher jump class but not a lower height class than his official measurement dictates. Different agility venues have different official jump height categories.

When agility was first established in England, and subsequently in continental Europe, Australia, the United States and Canada, all dogs were required to jump 30-inch hurdles and broad jumps up to 5 feet long and 15 inches high. Now, decades later, the sport has become so popular that height divisions are in place all over the world, with different countries and different venues following various jump height guidelines. Since the sport is still gaining popularity, it is probable that we will see further revision to the guidelines and the addition of even more jump height categories. The US is perhaps the country with the most agility venues and jump height options. We are lucky that agility is truly available here for any healthy dog.

Jump heights will always be a major issue in agility, because jumps are such a large part of the course. A standard competition course of 20 obstacles might include 13 jumps. Your dog will encounter jumps of widely varied colors, shapes, textures, material, motifs and dimensions. Teach him that, no matter what it looks like, he simply has to jump it if you say the word.

Some dogs are born jumpers and others are not, but even dogs that are not natural jumpers can learn to do it well. The first step is to have your dog's soundness evaluated; if his body is not sound, it will not hold up to the amount of jumping that an agility course demands.

While some types of dogs have an easier time with jumping than others, any sound dog can learn to jump.

The standard bar jump is the most common type of jump seen in agility trials.

The canine body type best suited to jumping is determined by how much weight must be carried per amount of supporting bone in the leg (see Ch. 1). In addition, the dog's physical structure and condition and his enjoyment of jumping all play an important part in determining how fit he is for jumping.

For agility, your dog needs to be strong enough in the rear to tuck his haunches under him like a coiled spring, compressed and then powered upward by the release of tension when he pushes off. Once over the jump, successful or not, his forequarters absorb all that pressure when he lands on the other side. The heavier your dog and the more powerful his spring, the more force his front end has to withstand on landing. That force is greatly intensified when an immediate sharp turn is required to get to the next obstacle.

The experienced dog, taking his directional cue from his handler, will actually be twisting in the air and assuming the new direction before he hits the ground. That means his inside leg, the one on the side toward the turn, will absorb nearly all the force of the landing. Because the leg will be turning as it hits the ground, a great deal of lateral strain will be put on the dog's shoulder, knee and pastern joints.

No matter how much strength the dog has both fore and aft, if he doesn't know where to begin his leap and at what angle or rotation he needs to propel himself, he will have problems jumping in agility. So a smart jumper is an efficient jumper— one that knows how to read a jump, bothers to do so and then puts out the right amount and kind of effort to clear it properly. An efficient jumper consistently turns in a clean performance in a faster time. More importantly, he lasts longer.

Although the first thing you usually wish for in jump training is a dog that bounds as though on springs, dogs that are spring-loaded don't always jump wisely or well. To be successful on an agility course, a dog needs good judgment about the height and depth of an upcoming jump and he needs to take off properly and propel himself accurately to clear the jump without wasting time and energy.

The impressive dogs that come to a standstill and then effortlessly pop over a jump are real crowd-pleasers, but they are not using their gifts to the fullest. Neither are the dogs that jump much higher than necessary. Some dogs even spring straight-legged over the jumps and look to be standing in the air, usually several inches above the jump. These are very talented dogs with very inefficient jumping styles.

Teaching your dog to jump is largely a matter of helping him develop timing and strength. When a dog is more powerful in the forequarters, he prefers to pull himself over things rather than propel from the rear. This shows up markedly in A-frame training when the dog wants to hop onto the obstacle and power up the ramp on his forequarters rather than using those rear muscles extensively. Assuming he doesn't suffer from hip dysplasia or another infirmity of the rear, this type of dog needs a conditioning program of road work and stair work, as well as the jumping exercises in this chapter, to develop his thigh muscles. His

The panel jump is seen at all levels of AKC agility but is not always seen in other flavors of agility.

forequarters will be able to handle what he learns to put out with his rear muscles.

The more dangerous long-term situation is seen in dogs with powerful hindquarters and much weaker structures in the front. These dogs usually have rear legs with very sharp angulation of the bones and a lot of muscle in their thighs. A line drawn from the ilium (broad upper portion of hipbone) to the rear foot, following the major bones of the leg, would result in a very pronounced zig-zag. In marked contrast, the angulation of the bones of their front legs is much less pronounced; that is, a line from the withers to the front foot through the major bones would be only slightly zig-zagged. These dogs, assuming that no shoulder problem or other infirmity of the front exists, can be strengthened with road work, digging, swimming and climbing.

Still, because of the structural imbalance between the front and the rear, the handler should beware of the dog's tendency to overstress his front and the damage that can be done over time, particularly to the shoulders. It's especially important that dogs of this physical type learn to judge their jumps and propel themselves smoothly with just enough power to clear the jump. All of that excess push from the rear makes for extra strain on the shock-absorbing front, and it will eventually cause damage.

Jump heights are calculated to be high enough for your dog to be challenged without requiring heroic effort. And, because there is so much variation between courses, your dog will turn as often in one direction as the other as he competes at different venues, cumulatively distributing the force evenly on both sides. The most important preparations for agility jumping are to have your dog in great shape physically and to help him maintain an enthusiasm and confidence for jumping as you guide his technical progress.

BAR JUMPS AND SOLID JUMPS

BAR JUMPS AND SOLID JUMPS INTRODUCTION

It's important to note here that solid jumps appear in AKC agility as panel jumps and in international agility as viaduct jumps and wall jumps. Most of the jumps in agility are bar jumps, consisting of two uprights (side-support stanchions) spanned by one or more bars of 4 to 5 feet long. The jumps might be as close as 12 feet apart in one part of the course and could be as much as 30 feet apart elsewhere. This variable spacing requires the dog to know his body well and adjust the length of his stride on the run. As handlers, we are always trying to find the best compromise between ground speed and tight turns for maximum efficiency over jumps. The dog charging straight ahead in full body extension is maximizing his ground speed, but turning tightly is impossible in this position. The dog must collect his hindquarters underneath him and tuck his body together in order to apply a rotational thrust to his takeoff if he is to turn tightly over a jump. This takes two interrelated skills: body awareness from the dog and timely information from the handler.

BAR JUMPS AND SOLID JUMPS PROGRESSION

STEP 1
- Jump bars, cone games and handling.
- Enjoy tandem jumping and work with assistant to accustom dog to jumping beside you and toward you.

Lay jump bars on the ground, amply but not evenly spaced, and trot your dog on leash over the bars. Use 6 to 10 bars over a distance of about 60 feet. Change the spacing after every couple of repetitions and present some bars at an angle rather than straight across. These simple jump lanes without stanchions are for fostering coordination and timing rather than

Cone games introduce skills that the dog will use on his approach to the various jumps.

strength, so they are equally appropriate for puppies and adult dogs. This exercise improves the dog's awareness for jumping in the same way that the ladder exercises improve the dog's awareness for ramp work.

Cone games combine the elements of sending, turning tightly and accelerating out of the turn. These are very important aspects of jumping success that require teamwork as well as training. The cone's shape defines a tight arc for the dog to follow. Click as he rounds the turn. Your well-conditioned pick-up finger is the target to which the dog returns for his reward.

To introduce cone games, start with the clicker in the hand next to the dog and the lure in your other hand, or your "new" hand, since you will be changing sides. At first, lure your dog around the cone with a toy or cookie and click as he passes the halfway point. Rotate into your dog, so you will tighten his turn even more by changing sides. Cheer and run away, letting your dog catch you for his reward. Get it? The goal is to inspire your dog to dig in and accelerate toward you after rounding the cone. The front cross maneuver (see Ch. 5) keeps him from drifting wide.

You can progress quickly with cone games to the point where you are sending the dog away from you to go around the cone or a tree, trash can or anything round and stationary. This should remain a fun game and not a chore. There is value in the sendaway skill, for sure, but the main focus of this game is the dog's own control of the tight turn and his digging in to accelerate all the way back to you. Run! Be fun!

This game is a terrific warm-up for working with jumps in simple front-cross drills. Pay attention to the dog's path, how he is planning his turn and coordinating his turn with his jump trajectory. Is he applying a rotation to his jumping on takeoff? That is the cone game shining through in his jump training, and you are on your way to smart, efficient jumping.

Tandem jumping is good for both of you. Your clicker can mark any point of the dog's trajectory, such as front-end liftoff or hind-end clearance, but be especially mindful of capturing your dog's face looking forward, intent on his work. The bad habit of wheeling around to look at you while jumping is easily prevented by careful clicking of good body posture now.

Your dog may be on or off leash. Use jump bars 5 feet long, and give your dog plenty of room. As with all other obstacles, work sometimes with your dog on the left and sometimes on the right.

Keep the jumps low, and don't interfere with the dog's jumping. Let him figure it out. At this point, jumping is just simple fun, for the attitude, coordination, timing and teamwork rather than for the muscles.

If jumping with your dog is not for you, use a helper to hold the dog on one side while you go to the other. If possible, step over the little jump rather than go around, since that helps your dog learn to do the same. Do use enticement to help your dog decide to make the effort, but don't order your dog to come or to jump until he loves this work. Instead, use the same sort of cajoling you used for the first step of open-tunnel work.

It's great to have a helper for early jump lessons. The helper holds the dog back, activating the opposition reflex by praising and keeping him tuned in to you across the jump. When you call, the helper lets go when the dog is committed to the jump. Click as he jumps and reward him each time. Keep it filled with fun and praise!

During early jump training, low jumps also belong indoors as part of daily life. Set up a little jump in a doorway or hallway where the dog will have to go over it many times a day. It should be set from 4 inches to 12 inches high, low enough to be stepped over by humans. This is to give the dog ongoing practice without any strain. It's fine if he trots over it instead of hopping over; that takes coordination and timing too.

A piece of plywood placed across a doorway makes a serviceable jump. A tension rod designed for doing chin-ups in doorways works well too. Just drape a towel over it at first to make it solid for visibility. Move the indoor jumps around and also vary the heights.

STEP 2	• Straddle jumps and sendaways. Begin at 12 or fewer inches high.
	• Dog starts close to straddle jump.
	• Click front-end liftoff at first and then click only hind-end clearance.
	• Use single jumps for sendaways as with cone game described earlier.
	• Add handling, changes of direction with front crosses and pick-ups.

To teach the skill of powering from the rear and being mindful of the legs, I recommend positive drilling on straddle jumps after Step 1 is completed. Have the dog wait right in front of a jump that is

No matter the agility venue, there are always class divisions based on height. Look at the difference between a bar jump for a large dog (ABOVE) and a small dog (BELOW).

half his height at the withers. Straddle the jump bar yourself. While inviting the dog to jump, tempt him with a favorite enticement held just on the other side. Click as his front feet clear the bar, and give him the reward as he lands on the other side. In the first repetition, it's OK if he raps the jump with his hind feet because it's his effort you're rewarding initially. Even if the bar falls on the first repetition, your attitude is simply "Great! Thanks for trying!"

Hold the enticement in your other hand and invite him to jump back over the bar. After one or a few repetitions, depending on your dog, it's time to up the ante to click hind-end, rather than front-end, clearance. Now only a clean jump will earn a click. Let your clicker do the talking—either click for a clean jump or do not click if his feet hit the bar— don't verbalize any disappointment! You get to be the good guy.

Note that this exercise is not good for young puppies that are still uncoordinated. A good rule of thumb is that if your pup is not yet nimble in the ladder obstacle, then he will not yet have the quick command of his muscles needed for straddle jumping. The ladder and plank games and the quick-turning cone game will give him these skills as he matures.

The straddle jump game is especially useful for dogs that need more practice picking their feet up over the jumps and pushing off with their hindquarters. Because the dog begins so close to the bar, he must snap his knees immediately and jump vertically, from the rear, with all his appendages tucked and tidy. Because he is following the lure, he will automatically turn toward you as he lands.

As he gets more proficient and eager, begin to reward him less often and of course only for clear jumps. There is no need to mention mistakes. Just cheerfully put the bar back in place instead of clicking. By using the clicker and not scolding his mistakes, you keep the dog interested and pleased with himself. This simple exercise has turned many a nervous jumper into a confident one.

By starting with the jump low and keeping your attitude light and supportive, the dog doesn't feel pressured. Raise the jump more gradually than you think is necessary. And it need not be parallel. Raise the bar at one end and not the other in order to make your dog more astute.

Straddle jumps are great for helping the dog discover his own strength as a jumper. Now it's time to add running to the jumping. You can practice sending your dog by using the jump just as you did the cone in Step 1, and you will be on your way to sendaway jump training. The dog takes the direction from your signal and then runs to perform the task on his own, digs in and turns sharply around the jump stanchion and accelerates back to you as you praise him.

When your dog is comfortable with this, begin raising the jump just a little at a time, depending on his ability and size. It's tempting to think that an extra couple of inches won't make any difference, but it often does; know your dog before you decide to raise the jump. We tend to think that jump height is the one variable we must change, but that is far from the whole picture! The other main variables that you should play with in this game include distance from dog to jump, his approach angle, the distance between you and your dog and performing the task on the run rather than from a standstill. With a supercharged dog it is often the handler's running that is the biggest distraction. It's important to keep this a high-energy game, keeping your dog's enthusiasm and confidence as you vary each of these factors.

Don't assume your dog is recalcitrant or thick-headed when he messes up with these simple jumps. As long as he's healthy, your dog can learn to jump,

The straddle jump game: clicking front-end (ABOVE) and hind-end (BELOW) clearance.

and jump well, if you let him begin where he is comfortable and gradually increase the challenge. If he's just not a natural jumper, there's nothing to be ashamed of. It's one of many things he can learn. With a little work you can have it all.

STEP 3

- Jump sequences. Use cavaletti if possible to encourage focus on bar. Start with lanes and circles.
- Click hind-end clearance and capture forward expression.
- Introduce multiple jumps, beginning at one-half dog's height and working up to his regulation jump height.
- Introduce jump squares with front crosses and pick-ups, then jump lanes and jump circles.
- Use pick-up lane and circle games after dog is comfortable and rhythmic in his jumping.

Now that your dog enjoys a working understanding of basic jumping, this practice should improve his timing and skill on the run. Start with cavaletti (round bars or rails attached to low stands) if possible, as they allow you to change the jump height just by rolling them over. They have no stanchions, so they are user friendly for the handler and they help focus the dog's attention on the jump bar itself. I prefer cavaletti that are 5 feet wide, and I often use them for puppies in a wheel configuration. Close to the center, the pup must pick his feet up quickly, and farther out he learns to extend his stride.

Agility is a sport in which the dog must learn to think and plan his jumping for himself. There is no anticipating where jumps will be placed on a competition course, what kind of obstacles will come immediately before and after the jumps and what sorts of turns and spacing will appear between them. It's quite common to face five or more different jumps in a row, so it's important that you give your dog ample exposure and practice to work out a personal jumping style that works jump after jump.

If your dog balks or goes under or around a jump, you shouldn't be working on this step yet. He needs more confidence. Play the cone game with two cones, sending your dog in a figure-8 around both cones for one click and treat. Then substitute jumps for the cones as in Step 2. This will help build the dog's mental stamina for multitasking.

A jump square is simply four jumps, all facing out from the center, forming a square if viewed from above. In this configuration introduce the idea of turning to a jump on either side rather than continuing to the jump straight ahead. This is easy to set up at home and should be done with your front cross pick-up game from the cone work in Step 1. This game helps your dog enjoy heeding your directions as well as getting over the jumps.

Jump lanes allow the dog to stretch out and enjoy the feeling of going over the succession of jumps down the line. Start with the jumps low and amply spaced, but not evenly spaced. This needs to be a conceptual task and not a ritual use of the dog's body. Because of the unpredictable layout of agility courses, his brain and body need to be comfortable making adjustments while he's moving. Vary your position: alongside the jumps, at the other end and calling the dog to you or running while the dog is running (this is the hardest variable for the wild-child dogs).

Jump circles allow the dog to jump around a perimeter, clockwise or counterclockwise. The handler generally keeps to the middle. Start with a "speed circle," which allows the dog to stretch out and jump without interruption.

Once your dog is comfortable and proficient with his jumping in these different patterns, reintroduce the front cross pick-up games as a positive way to keep the dog happy and quick while you change his path and redirect him on the run.

When should you raise the jump heights? You can start to do this as soon as the dog is comfortable and proficient with the set you've designed. I like to raise one or two jumps at a time, making the jump heights uneven, because it sharpens the dog's ability to judge each jump independently. After all, the ground is not perfectly level and therefore the equipment will not always be level. Your dog needs to be smart as well as happy while jumping!

SPREAD JUMPS

A spread jump has both height and depth. The triple jump consists of three bars set progressively higher from front to back. The double jump is sometimes seen with parallel top bars and sometimes as an ascending spread. The broad jump is low with more depth. When you ask your dog to jump a spread jump, you are asking him to reach out far and stretch his body long. He has to use his rear muscles forcefully to propel himself over a spread jump, and he should lengthen his running stride and extend his body to take the jump smoothly.

It takes more skill and more strength, but once your dog can judge these spread variations and coordinate his body back and forth between the compact body positioning required for tight turns and the full extension called for by the spread jumps, he will add a new dimension of fluidity to his jumping. His performance over various kinds of jumping challenges in sequence will begin to look smooth, efficient and powerful on the run. When the path is straight ahead, he will be able to jump any jump with great power, taking off from a greater distance away, flattening his arc a bit and landing farther past the jump on the run. When the path calls for a tight turn, he will shift his center of gravity back and take off closer to the jump, applying the appropriate rotational thrust to his take-off, so as to be turning already in the new correct direction on landing. When this savvy style is brought to all aspects of the dog's jumping, the combination of speed and efficient path will give him a faster time.

You needn't wait until your dog is jumping his regulation height to introduce some spread jumps. Once your dog's attitude and timing are well in place over low poles, it's good to introduce some jumps with depth. It will teach him to notice and gauge the all-important back bar of a jump along with its height. He should be enjoying jumping single poles at half his height or more and judging them accurately in order to be ready for an introduction to the spread jumps.

Many dogs have particular trouble negotiating spread jumps, especially the triple jump. When dogs have trouble with spread jumps, it is usually because they are confusing the two elements of difficulty, height and depth. Very commonly, a dog that otherwise jumps well will have a problem with the triple jump because the dog jumps to the same height he always jumps (perhaps showing a lack of variability in his jump training). His focus is on jumping the first bar; therefore, the apex of his jump trajectory is over that low bar and consequently he is on the descent when going over the higher rear bar. That is inadequate to the task, and his fundamentals need work.

Whatever combination of teaching aids your dog needs, you can find a trick that helps make it click for him. Keep your agility eyes open and find a solution that both you and your dog will enjoy. People have used everything from chicken wire between the boards to yanking their dogs through the air to get them to clear spread jumps cleanly. Beware of quick and dirty fixes like that. You are not well served teaching avoidance of the jumps!

You and your dog will be much happier if you teach the concept of adding the horizontal jumping component to the vertical component he already knows. It's a lot smarter and more fun to work on invitations to jump long rather than punishments for jumping short. You will also make your dog a much more clever jumper by teaching these concepts. It is certainly the clever brain rather than the worried brain that will save the day for you when your run is pushed to the utmost. Here is how to teach spread jumps so that your dog will understand them conceptually and not be fooled.

TRIPLE JUMP PROGRESSION

STEP 1	• Back bar is set to maximum of 12 inches high. • Straddle bars and bring dog very close to jump, as in bar jump Step 2. • Point out back bar and entice as with earlier straddle jump work.

Use opposition reflex collar work to show your dog the back bar without letting him jump. Tap on the bar with your free hand and ask the dog, "Is that your jump? Wanna jump? Good boy, there's your jump!" I'm sure you get the idea. It's important to rev him up, using the jump word he loves, and it's equally important not to let him throw himself on top of the bars. With your hand still in the collar, bring your enticement into play and make the dog ready, then let go. Immediately invite him to jump, and use the lure to draw a generous trajectory over the back bar. This is very much like the previous straddle jump work you did, but the dog must focus on the back bar. The fact that he is stationed very close to the jump means that his head is over the front bar, so it is not difficult to put his attention on the back bar, and that is the only bar you mention to him.

STEP 2	• Gradually raise bars and increase spread between them. • Stand beside jump.

If your dog is large, you will soon need to straddle just the back bar rather than straddle all of the bars and simply lean your weight to the back. At each new height, hold the collar again and spend a moment revving up the dog while tapping the back bar. Then let go and invite him to follow the lure as you draw the rounded trajectory over the back bar. The dog is a bit farther back from the jump as you raise the height to 16 inches and higher, but still he

The three bars of the triple jump are set lowest to highest, requiring the dog to judge both depth and height.

201

is close enough to the jump that you can see him looking at the back bar. With the previous straddle work you did with single-bar jumps and solid jumps, you know that your dog is mentally prepared and strong enough to clear the jump from this close distance.

When you feel he's ready for more freedom, position yourself beside the jump rather than between the bars. Put yourself alongside the back bar to keep that emphasis, and continue to mark that bar.

Some dogs come to agility having an advanced background in obedience. If your dog understands the obedience broad jump and doesn't seem to take to the other spread jumps, try setting broad jump boards beneath the triple jump poles for awhile. This could help your obedience dog see the similarity and apply the skills he knows to this new challenge. Many advanced obedience dogs have made the transition to agility spreads this way; use your own judgment, as every dog varies.

STEP 3
- Wean from lure and use clicker.
- Wean from tapping back bar.
- Vary handler position.
- Add low triple jump to jump lanes and circles.

You may have felt you did not have enough hands on the earlier steps, but now your dog needs to be taking over the job of focusing on the back bar and jumping over that bar, regardless of your position. Your main job remains to focus your dog on the back bar and use your clicker to mark the apex of the dog's trajectory over that bar. Perhaps at first you'll click front-end clearance of the back bar, but eventually it is hind-end clearance you want. Add all of the variables mentioned earlier, including distance, angle of approach and motion.

DOUBLE JUMP PROGRESSION

STEP 1
- Double jump set no higher than 12 inches.
- Straddle jump with center halfway between the two bars.
- Focus dog on back bar and lure as with triple jump.

In the USDAA agility the double jump is presented with ascending bars for small dogs and parallel dogs for larger dogs; in AKC agility the double jump has parallel top bars for all dogs. With ascending bars, the obstacle is trained just like the triple jump. The greater challenge comes with parallel top bars, whereby the dog must notice the back bar and then reach his apex halfway between the two top bars.

Straddle-jump work is good for the double jump. Because the apex of the proper jump trajectory will be halfway between the two bars, you should position yourself midway. However, go through the motions of holding the dog's collar and tapping the back bar, as with the triple jump, to make sure that the dog notices the breadth of the obstacle. Now invite your dog to follow the lure as you draw the desired trajectory over both bars.

STEP 2
- Gradually raise bars.
- Stand beside jump.

Position yourself beside the midpoint between the two top bars. As before, your dog needs to begin a bit farther away from the jump as the height is raised, but do not give him a running start. It's only a bit of start-up leeway. He still needs to be looking for that back bar, and you need to keep emphasizing the bigger trajectory that it takes to encompass the wider jump.

STEP 3	• Wean from lure. Use clicker. • Wean from tapping back bar. • Vary handler position. • Play cone games with low double jumps. • Add low double jumps to jump circles.

Weaning from the lure and employing your clicker for front-end clearance and then hind-end clearance goes quickly now that the dog has so much experience with the clicker.

It is very helpful to the dog for you to show him a low double jump in the spirit of the very familiar cone games you have played so often with the single jumps. Now, while you are working this advanced session with the double jump, is a good time to take advantage of an angled approach to make your dog very smart about recognizing a parallel double jump on the run. When you surprise your dog with a triple jump in a jump lane, you know that he will see the depth of the jump because of the ascending bars. But if you simply add a parallel double jump to a jump lane, your dog might not notice the depth in time, and that could make him insecure. This game is better as an early on-the-run exercise. When you play the cone game with an angled approach he will get a good look at the depth of the obstacle from the side as he steps in to jump it with the rotation he knows to apply on cone games. Then add a low double jump to a small-diameter jump circle, where again the dog will have a more rounded approach to the jump and therefore will get a chance to recognize the depth of the obstacle.

After several such presentations, your dog will be much more likely to recognize a double jump, even head-on, because he'll be looking for depth.

The dog must learn to recognize the double jump, with its parallel top bars, to distinguish it from the similar-looking single bar jump.

And he will also have a lot of treats in his bank account of confidence, so that even when he does make a mistake, he will just shake it off and fix it.

BROAD JUMP PROGRESSION

STEP 1	• One broad-jump board, stood upright on one of its long sides. • Click hind-end clearance of board. Very few repetitions. • Add second board, in proper horizontal position with lower side toward dog, behind and touching upright board. • Click hind-end clearance. Very few repetitions.

Putting the first board on its end helps the dog see this obstacle as a vertical challenge rather than a ramp to be walked. Using these first boards as straddle jumps helps ensure that your dog jumps over without touching the boards. You could also jump the jump with your dog to inspire him to lift over it. Use your imagination. If your dog is very small, use a strong lure and draw a big trajectory over the boards in order to inspire the dog to jump long and horizontally. This is a big obstacle for a tiny dog!

STEP 2

- Lay upright board flat for total of two horizontal boards.
- Add a wingless jump across the middle between the two boards. Several repetitions.
- Move jump bar to the back of the last board.

The wingless jump bar helps remind the dog to jump rather than to step on the boards. It should be just high enough to invite sufficient vertical liftoff to clear the two boards in a natural bascule. The dog's focus should be primarily on the bar, and clearance of the two boards is largely incidental. After a session or two you should move the jump

The broad jump requires a different type of training, focusing on distance rather than height.

bar to the back of the obstacle in order to help the dog focus on the back board rather than the front or the middle.

Broad jumps in competition are marked by tall posts at each corner. The dog must jump between the poles and clear the entire length of the jump to avoid faults. Using the jump bar to help your dog focus correctly on the back board of the broad jump also gives him a familiarity with these marker posts as a cue to remind him of what he must do on this obstacle.

For very small dogs, two boards will compose the regulation obstacle. Continue to inspire long jumping and click only hind-leg clearance of the last board. Gradually lower and then remove the jump bar. For larger dogs, it's time to add another board.

STEP 3
- Add third board, placed upright as before, in front of two horizontal boards. Place jump bar at back of obstacle.
- Raise jump bar proportionately as you add more depth to jumping effort.
- After one or two short sessions, lay first board flat for total of three horizontal boards. Then lower jump bar gradually as above.

The jump bar needs to command the dog's attention toward the back of the obstacle, just as he must focus on the back bar of a triple jump in order to gauge it correctly. When your third board is moved from vertical to horizontal, the jump bar at the back should be about 16 inches high. As your dog accepts the challenge and enjoys the long trajectory, you will need to lower the jump bar gradually and continue to inspire your dog to jump long without touching the boards. One way to do this is to run with your dog and have a big celebration after he clears the last board! For large dogs, it's now time to add more boards.

STEP 4

- Add fourth board, placed upright, in front of three horizontal boards. Place jump bar at back of obstacle.
- Hold dog's collar and tap jump bar to focus his attention there before jumping.
- When all is well with this effort, lay first board horizontally for a total of four boards.
- For large dogs, after a session or two at this depth, add fifth and final board to front in upright position. Lay board flat after several good repetitions.

The obstacle now is beginning to look like a long wide ramp, so it would be a good strategy to hold the dog's collar and tap the jump bar again, talking excitedly about the bar being a good thing to jump. This is very much like triple-jump work, also designed to focus the dog on the back of the jump. After successful repetitions, lay the fourth board horizontally and raise the jump bar up to 18–20 inches. When the fifth and final board is finally laid horizontally, the jump bar at the back will be at least 20 inches high, and the joy in jumping horizontally while running all out should be emphasized.

It's very important to continue to click hind-end clearance of the last board in order to keep the dog mindful of keeping his legs up in the air. It's tempting to click at the apex of the dog's trajectory or at the middle of the obstacle, but this is too soon for the many dogs that tend to dip the inside leg when turning. It is important to clear all of the boards cleanly without touching any.

When you're ready to begin including a broad jump in your jump sequences, give a little extra room between jumps at first. It will take some practice for your dog to get the knack of stretching long over the broad jump and then immediately coiling for a taller jump. It's very helpful to set up a downscaled series closer together specifically for working on this flexibility. Once he's comfortable, it's time to incorporate turns as well, both left and right, also using simplified jumps at first. Think of the three Ds, and add those elements of distraction, distance and duration to your training as you and your dog advance in skill and teamwork.

JUMPS SUMMARY

STEP 1: Cone games. Vary solid jumps at low heights indoors, so dog hops over routinely. Tandem jumping with your dog over low and uneven bars is a plus. If your dog seems uncoordinated, go back to the ladder work from the introduction to ramps for the proprioceptive work of finding and coordinating all four feet in a confined space.

STEP 2: Straddle-jump exercises are part of early jumping work because they foster the ability to turn while jumping and the mindfulness to keep all four feet out of the way in tight spots.

STEP 3: Introduce multiple low single jumps in simple configurations like circles, ovals and lanes. Use ample but variable spacing to encourage the dog to extend and collect his body as he adapts to the variations. Introduce spread jumps and broad jumps. Focus the dog's attention on the back bar or board at each step.

STEP 4: Incorporate all types of familiar jumps into more challenging jump sequences. Give more space before and after spreads until the dog gains skill in extending and compressing his body for the more horizontal and more vertical jumping efforts. As always, vary your variables!

CHAPTER 9

The Pause Table

The pause table is a sturdy 3-foot-square structure with a textured flat-top surface. The height of the table varies according to the jump height class. The dog must get onto the table, assume the down position and pause; the

Genius is eternal patience.
—Michelangelo

pause must be maintained in competition for five seconds. The judge begins counting backward from five as the dog assumes the correct position, counting aloud in a cadence, "five, four, three, two, one, go." Any dog that breaks position must put himself back correctly, and then the count either resumes or begins again, according to the level of the class.

In the excitement of competition, a dog often finds it difficult to tolerate this sudden interruption of the course run. A dog that will stay put while his

When released, the dog must be ready to spring from the table and resume full speed.

handler moves away makes it much easier for the handler to be in place to direct him through the next sequence.

Many agility dogs, fast or slow, take singular exception to the "hurry up and wait" requirement of this obstacle. For that reason, I introduce the release word first. That is, I teach my dogs the command to "go" before I emphasize the command to "wait." I backchain the correct performance. This lets me maintain an enthusiastic attitude and the playful nature of the game rather than emphasizing the downtime aspect. Try it! This is the same strategy I use very successfully when teaching my dogs to stay at the start line while I lead out. Whether you're training for a solid table performance or a solid start-line performance, this is a very effective approach that accomplishes the reliable stay and the explosive takeoff, all without an argument.

PAUSE TABLE INTRODUCTION

When a dog performs the pause table perfectly, it's done in one smooth motion. By the time the dog is completely on the table, he has already assumed the correct position.

It is unusual when a dog can learn the whole job at once and learn it well. Many dogs feel resistant to what they view as an imposition in the context of running agility obstacles. A dog that is expected to put it all together too soon may become patterned for a slow and deliberate performance, which is not at all what you want.

If you try to put the whole picture together when any of the elements are less than foolproof, you create problems that will cost you a lot of time and extra work to reshape. The steps outlined here are perfected separately and then brought together.

Competitors with large dogs will find that the taller table actually makes the job easier. Though we will always see an occasional dog of any size go sailing onto the table and off the opposite side (incurring a penalty in competition), this happens less often when the dog has to jump up as well as forward onto the table.

PAUSE TABLE PROGRESSION

STEP 1
- Make dog comfortable with table.
- Introduce release word.
- After he loves game, introduce table command and send him.

Before introducing a command for the table, let your dog get comfortable there. Even if your dog is apt to hop onto strange things before checking them out, it doesn't hurt to introduce the table by getting up there yourself and inviting your dog to join you. Being on the table with your dog helps prevent a tendency for him to jump on and off and on again. Right from the beginning, he will tend to hop up and stay there if you are up there with him, so it's helpful for the overeager dog as well as the hesitant one. As with any new experience, downscale to an easier Step 1 if necessary. If your dog needs to start with a lower table or a larger platform, that's fine. Just work your way gradually to the real thing and use your imagination to help him associate it with pleasure. From there, it's easy to have him hop up without you.

At first, don't put any emphasis on making your dog assume a particular position on the table. As you play with him up there, he learns to love being there. Once he loves this silly game, it's time to add a command. The first command isn't the command to get on or the command to assume a position, it's the command to "go!" Whether your release signal will be a physical cue or a verbal cue, give the command and immediately run to the reinforcement. Be it treats

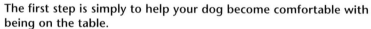

The first step is simply to help your dog become comfortable with being on the table.

or a tug toy, give the release cue and then bolt, in that order. The game is "Go!" and, as the handler, you must play it correctly or else the dog will not be honoring your cue. Soon we'll add the game of exactly when to go.

Once your dog loves the table and his explosive release game, begin to send him to the table from farther away. Now you may name the obstacle. Reward him for getting onto the table, and then issue the release command and reward him for that as well. This step is completed when your dog runs and jumps onto his regulation-size table with glee. If you've done your backchaining well, Step 1 does not take long. Because we are not requiring a particular position, do not stay long on this step. Move on to Step 2 as soon as you have established the joyful attitude and quick performance you want on the send and release.

STEP 2

(See also Step 3 for concurrent exercise)
- Send dog to table.
- Have rapid-fire, active and cheerful click-and-treat session, starting with any behaviors dog offers, and then free-shape down (and sit if you will be participating in AKC agility competition; UKC agility offers the option of sit or down on the table).

Your student hops on and performs for a coveted reward, hops off when you release him and observes your neutral behavior toward him while he is on the ground. Performing on the table is what energizes you and produces clicks and toys or goodies for him. Repeat this exercise a few times during each session. As your dog becomes quick at it, begin to vary the angle from which you send him. Gradually increase your distance from the table if he is ready for you to work on a lead-out (meaning that you walk toward the next obstacle while he remains on the table).

This step is to serve as an intermediate level of progress for the dog. At first the table is a place he goes to "get good stuff." Ultimately the table will become an object that he must "get on, do as you're told and stay there until told otherwise." That's a big jump in responsibility. This step allows the progress to occur gradually, so that the dog can assume more responsibility without such a big leap. This is a temporary step designed to cement the dog's positive attitude while increasing his responsibility.

STEP 3

- Away from pause obstacle, perfect dog's instant response to down command (See Section I, Obedience for Agility, Down, for the best way to shape this instant down).
- Once he is quick as a wink, introduce "wait" by delaying click.
- Introduce verbal praise marker to bridge between position and click (this is called a "keep going" signal).
- Introduce distractions and practice everywhere.

This should be such a great game that the dog should be diving headlong into the down position whenever you begin the cue. If he is waiting for you to "assume the position," then you are not making the game enough fun. You want to recognize and praise him for anticipating the cue during this step. Have your clicker ready! The dog that ignores his handler about assuming the down on the table is the dog who needs separate work on assuming the down anytime and anywhere. Begin by reviewing the basic commands in Chapter 2, both at home and in public. This is all part of the necessary groundwork.

Don't combine practicing the down with a pause obstacle until your dog really enjoys the down command and is quick about it. Many handlers who use the pause table for early training sessions with the down find that they have inadvertently

CHAPTER 9: The Pause Table

patterned their dogs for resistance and slow responses there, even after the dogs become quick at responding to the command elsewhere. Better to perfect a fast response off the table first and then transfer that familiar game to the table.

Through your quick response to the dog's correct action when you say the command word, you show him how to train you to reward him faster. Training your dog to be operant is a different sort of job, and it requires a different mindset. This training will prevent you from intimidating a sensitive dog or from setting up a power struggle with a tough dog. If you escalate force training to combat his so-called stubbornness, you may set up a sullen passive disobedience. Where a more confident dog would actively resist, the quieter dog withdraws. In either case, letting the dog control the more advanced fine-tuning of this exercise brings out a cooperative spirit.

When your dog is hitting the deck with speed on your down command, make him start waiting a second longer before you click and reward him. It's a gradual process. Begin by interspersing immediate clicks with slightly delayed clicks. As always, don't move the treat until after you have clicked. The gradual delay of the click is what shapes the "wait" game. If your dog has been trained that "stay" is a lengthy exercise, or that he should flop over onto one hip or tuck a paw, you might prefer a different command because you will want your dog to remain ready to run while in the pause position. In agility, commands and signals can be repeated and used together. Even if you train your dog in practice to be steady with a single command, you are free to repeat the command and/or hold a signal during the exercise in competition when nerves are tighter.

Good signals can be much stronger than words. An upraised arm or a palm outstretched toward the dog can help keep him steady. Although you need to keep eye contact with the dog in early pause

This Bull Terrier obliges his handler with a down on the pause table, but he can't wait to get back to the action!

training, you do not ultimately want the dog to rely on that to keep him steady. You will need to focus momentarily on the next obstacle, prior to the judge's release, in preparation for continuing on the course.

Many intent dogs will pop up in anticipation when their handlers look away from them. You need to train your dog to stay while you move your head and even walk away. The clicker is the perfect tool for this step.

STEP 4

- Introduce the down command on table.
- Send dog and begin to sharpen timing so as to effect an instant down.
- Use clicker to mark position.
- When you begin to delay click in order to perfect "wait" element, bridge gap with verbal marker such as "Good boy!"
- Gradually your release word substitutes for click.

When your dog is happy to go to the table on command, and also happy and fast with the instant down everywhere else, it's time to put the two together. This step is much like Step 2 except that you will have your dog assume a position every time he hops onto the pause table. Keeping the joy of the game, delay your release for varying amounts of time, but continue to mark the correct position with a word of praise. Keep your dog fast on the departure by releasing him precisely and with high energy. In general, crimes of action are easier to correct in agility than are crimes of inaction.

This process of putting it all together, progressing from a handler-centered interaction to a dog-centered interaction, takes time. Build a good foundation for your table performance by training and perfecting each element of difficulty separately and keeping each piece of the behavior strong through variable reinforcement.

STEP 5
- Continue to strengthen down/stay and sit/stay on the table using the "push me" and tug games.
- Introduce distractions, wet and slippery tables and odd approach and departure angles.

Just as you increased gradually and variably the length of time your dog had to wait for his reward when you were teaching the instant down, now incorporate variable extensions of time between the position and release on the table. Every once in a while, pull out a motivating idea or two and toss them in again to keep things lively.

This is a great time to introduce some playful "push the dog" games while he is performing on the table. Of course you must start by pushing gently, as if to push him off balance, and click when he tries to stabilize himself against you.

Play tug games on the table. Nothing is better for helping your dog learn the physics of inertia and centrifugal force. As you let go and he has to rebalance, click and reward. If he falls off or jumps off, game over. This means that if your dog would take the toy and run, you must play this table game on leash. It soon becomes such a fun experience for your dog that if he does fall off, he will immediately jump back on in order to get you to play again! That's what you want, a dog that fights to stay on the table rather than letting himself slide off. The good stuff happens up there, and the reward for fighting to stay on is worth playing this fun game.

Because you've maintained a kinetic pace at the table, never making your dog stay long, he should be patterned to expect an energetic release, which he demonstrates by remaining fully prone, looking at you. If you see him lean back and get comfortable, either you're increasing the stay time too much at once or your energy is waning. The trick is to keep your dog's interest while you keep him steady longer and longer. Work up to ten seconds or more, and it doesn't matter how many weeks it takes you to get there. Your dog's attitude and accuracy have come together now, and lengthening the time he can hold the position will be a matter of reading your dog correctly and keeping him motivated.

Don't forget to work with your dog on your left and on your right, so he can turn either clockwise or counterclockwise on the table. Introduce wet tables and slippery ones. Then add the pause table to your obstacle sequences to complicate the well-taught components. Keep in mind the many unexpected variables your dog will have to bear in mind in order to learn to handle different pause tables well.

PAUSE TABLE SUMMARY
STEP 1: Make your dog comfortable on obstacle with you. Introduce high-energy release cue. Introduce table command and begin to send dog to table.

STEP 2: Introduce click-and-treat sessions on pause table. Incorporate down (and sit if desired) via free-shaping to ensure dog's operant participation.

STEP 3: Perfect instant down away from pause obstacle. Shape "wait" by delaying click and introduce verbal marker for position as "keep-going" signal to keep the behavior strong. Introduce distractions.

STEP 4: Combine instant down with pause obstacle. Vary length of time your dog must wait. Release cue from Step 1 replaces click.

STEP 5: Introduce distractions. Play tug and "push-the-dog" games. Introduce angled approaches and departures. Introduce wet and slippery conditions. Add pause table to obstacle sequences.

Depending on the flavor of agility, a sit or down may be required on the pause table.

The Weave Poles

No obstacle calls for pure agility like the weave poles. This obstacle consists of 6 to 12 poles, approximately 1 inch in diameter, spaced 18 to 24 inches apart depending on the flavor of agility (AKC, UKC, NADAC, etc.) you are enjoying. The dog must enter the row of poles from the right (that is to say, with the first pole on his left). Then he must weave back and forth, slalom-style, down the line. Any deviation, including beginning on the wrong side of the first pole, popping out of the poles or skipping any pole, is incorrect.

> *The greater the obstacle, the more glory in overcoming it.*
> —Jean Baptiste Moliere

There are many effective approaches to teaching agility dogs to weave. Obviously we want to pattern the dog for accuracy and speed and give him an unabashed enjoyment of this nonsensical task we

The set-up for Step 1 with poles and two ex-pens.

call weaving. Top agility dogs can weave 12 poles in two seconds!

Speed comes more readily when the dog is happy, so use all of your tricks to keep him working tail-up. As the task approaches regulation difficulty and the dog has to flex sharply, make the extra effort on each step to keep the work fun and snappy. This job is a lot to remember, so you must always gauge your dog's current frame of mind and level of competence. Bolster his speed and confidence by reviewing previous steps occasionally. Some lithe-bodied canine athletes go through these steps quickly and are weaving regulation poles in days, but most dogs take weeks to put all the steps together at speed. The approach we will discuss here, the channel method, calls for the dog to run a channel—a column formed by two rows of individual weave poles. It requires two sets of six channel-style poles. We will also use two ordinary eight-panel exercise pens (ex-pens) that are anywhere from 2 to 3 feet tall.

WEAVE POLE PROGRESSION

STEP 1	• One set of six channel poles spread at least 12 inches apart to form roomy column down the middle. • One ex-pen is used to form a three-sided box from poles 1 to 3 and from poles 3 to 5. • Last two panels of ex-pen form exit at pole 6. • Second ex-pen is used on other side to form entrance at pole 1 and boxes from poles 2 to 4 and from poles 4 to 6.

If you are using an assistant, take advantage of the principle of "eager restraint." The helper motivates your dog and praises him for pulling toward you, even while holding the dog back. We want the dog to pull forward into the channel and toward you. The ex-pens ensure his correct path, so he doesn't have to worry about his performance, only about getting to you and his reward. The channel poles are staggered, with the first pole on the dog's left. This is very important for helping your dog feel the pattern of always entering a line of weave poles with the first pole on his left. Entice your dog and call him; your helper then releases the dog to run to you. If no helper is available, simply lure your dog down the line, clicking and treating while he is in the channel.

Step 1 relies on the ex-pen props to get the job done accurately. The dog simply runs the channel. The dog is introduced to channel either by luring, by clicking and treating while in channel or with the aid of a helper, as in introductory tunnel work. After a couple of good fast repetitions, begin to click only as the dog's nose passes the last pole, because now he can see that he has run them all.

Once the dog is happily running down the wide channel, move the two rows closer together until the channel is 6 inches wide. Now the dog will begin to swish a bit from side to side as he runs the line. Only Step 1 uses two ex-pens and such a wide channel. Do not spend too long on this step after your dog has mastered it with full speed. Step 1 is complete when your dog is fast and happy running the 6-inch channel by himself with you at the end or the beginning, beside him on either side, ahead or behind him, and you are clicking only for correct exit. You can vary his approach angle to ensure that he can find the entry from either side. Then go on to Step 2, which lets the dog take on some responsibility.

When one ex-pen is removed, the handler initially positions herself on the side of the dog without the ex-pen.

STEP 2	• One set of six channel poles with channel 6 inches wide and only one ex-pen in place, from poles 1 to 3 and 3 to 5, as in Step 1.
	• Shape performance independent of handler position, as in Step 1.
	• Wean from clicking each box to a click only for correct exit and establish verbal marker for correct entry.
	• Use target stick to reinforce correct entry.
	• Name obstacle.

Now the job is open to operant conditioning, and the dog can choose to "weave." Stand with the dog on your left at pole 1 and click when he goes forward into the ex-pen box. Treat as he weaves toward you; repeat with the next box, clicking as he weaves away from you and treating as he weaves toward you. Then click for correct exit as above. Use the treats low and along the dog's path so he keeps his head low and is in position to continue weaving. Really celebrate with your last click, and treat as the dog exits correctly. Then go back the other way, with the dog on your right. Make sure to click as the dog goes away from you, not when he comes back; this keeps him facing the work rather than looking up at you while he is weaving.

Now is a good time to polish the dog's understanding of correct weave entry. Use a target stick to accomplish this. Touching the stick is a simple click-and-treat parlor trick. Bringing this trick to the weave poles helps the dog think of his entry without looking for his handler's position. The ex-pen ensures that your dog will approach the stick with the first weave pole on his left. Keep the target low, between poles 1 and 2, click/treat the touch and then let your dog follow the stick down the short channel. Of course it's also important that you vary your own position and stance in order to make the dog's choice

The handler's position on the outside of the ex-pen makes weaving a bit more difficult.

independent of you. Let the target stick between poles 1 and 2 cue the dog, and the ex-pen will ensure his success.

Once the dog is performing quickly and happily, introduce an audible marker for correct entry, which will become your dog's "keep-going" signal. As the dog enters correctly, make your marker sound and do not follow with a treat. Click for the next box and give a high-value treat. For the next few repetitions in each direction, employ your marker for entry and be quick to click as the dog goes away from you into the next box. Treat now! The dog's performance will get faster.

Now it's time to eliminate the click at the second box and only click for correct exit. Use your marker at entry and click/treat with a big party at the exit. When your dog understands and is diving into this game to make you click, it's time to name the obstacle. Remember, don't name any obstacle until your dog enjoys it.

As your dog becomes faster and more determined in his performance, vary your handler position by moving ahead or waiting behind on either side while he is working this short set. No matter what your own movement is, always use your entry marker and exit click correctly. Don't be late just because you are not beside your dog, as he needs quick information as you continue to complicate his job. Any mistake on his part simply doesn't earn a click. End the repetition cheerfully and try again.

STEP 3	• Two sets of six channel poles with ex-pens on one side; each set is channel of 6 inches wide, and the two sets are about 15 feet apart. • Use marker for entry and click/treat for exit on each set, but do both sets in a row. Repeat down and back. • Move sets to 10 feet apart. Interrupt sets with treat as before, then send dog ahead to second set. • When dog is fast and happy with game, impatient to get to second set of poles, decrease distance to 5 feet between sets and continue from first to second set without a click/treat in between, only after. • Now put two sets together to form one set of 12 poles in a 6-inch channel with ex-pens on one side. Mark correct entry and click/treat celebration for correct exit at 12th pole.

Send your dog ahead of you to let him choose the correct entry for himself. Mark the correct entry with your marker sound. Click the correct exit and step in with a great treat as you move to the second set of poles. Backhand the treat from the hand next to the dog to keep both of you facing straight ahead.

Send your dog ahead to the second set of poles and mark his entry, and then really celebrate as you click/treat his exit. Don't move the two sets closer together just because your dog can accomplish them; move them because the dog demands more! He should be showing off with his poles, not tolerating them. Be sure you are inspiring confidence.

STEP 4

- Two sets of six poles in 6-inch-wide channels with ex-pens on one side. Sets moved to 15 feet apart again.
- Vary width of channels by making a V from 6 inches at entry to 3 inches at exit on first set, then from 3 inches at entry to 6 inches at exit on the second set. Add front and rear crosses between the two sets of poles.
- Wean to regulation in-line poles (closed channels) on both sets.
- Close the distance between the two sets in increments as in Step 3.

This is the transition from swishing to true weaving. You've only got inches to go before the poles are in a straight line, but these last inches might take many times the work of the earlier steps.

It makes for a smarter weaving dog to change channel width unevenly. My favorite way to keep the dog at full speed while making the channel narrower is to leave the first set's entry at 6 inches wide but move the exit on the 6th pole set to 3 inches wide. The dog's momentum from the familiar entry carries him successfully through the more difficult last poles. Then he is paid for his genius between the sets. Add a front cross here, then send him ahead again to the second set. He might look carefully at the narrower entry on the second set, but soon understands it and relaxes as the job becomes easy again toward the exit. Soon he is diving in and driving ahead through both sets just as before.

This photo illustrates correct weave pole entry at speed.

Now you can add a rear cross at the second set, remaining behind as he enters.

Now narrow the channel to 3 inches throughout. When the dog is as fast as before, leave the first entry at 3 inches wide but narrow the exit of the first set to regulation difficulty. Narrow the entry of the second set to regulation and leave the exit at 3 inches wide. When you front cross and come back the other way, the dog's experience is the same on your other side. The entry and exit are softened, but the middle, where he gets a treat while the sets are far enough apart, is more difficult. If you can go directly from 3 inches wide to regulation, that is fine. If your dog keeps his speed and confidence better by going from 3 inches to 2 inches, etc., that is also fine. There is no need to rush this, and there are many variables to manipulate.

Once you start working with your channels this narrow, the dog's job begins getting more difficult.

Regulation weave poles are set in a straight line with no channel between them.

Keep him motivated with quick success, enticements and lots of praise and excitement. Don't be disappointed in mistakes, just end the repetition and run, don't walk, to try again. Work with drive. Perform a few repetitions at a time, then enjoy a break.

If your dog makes repeated mistakes, look at what you are doing. Are you crowding him? Are you driving too hard forward while he is thinking about his entry, thereby pushing him past it with your pressure? He has too little experience to fight you for the correct space; be respectful of his need to think! It is still best to let him enter ahead of you, as in Step 3. That is a skill he will always need. He does not yet need to be trained to enter behind you. He needs to trust his own brain about putting the first pole on his left and rocking back at speed in order to secure correct entry on his own.

This step is completed when your dog can negotiate quickly and happily, without your guidance (or misguidance), from either end and from either side, a row of 12 regulation weave poles with the ex-pens in place on one side.

STEP 5

- Off with the ex-pens! Begin by moving ex-pens just a few inches away from poles and gradually increase space between ex-pen and pole. In only a few sessions ex-pens are no longer physical cues for the dog.
- When ex-pens are removed, separate poles into two regulation sets of six poles and add front and rear crosses between sets, clicking and treating a few times.
- Put sets together and put front and rear crosses before and after the set of 12 regulation poles.

This step is much fun, with so many variables to vary! But don't vary too many at once. It's exciting to see your dog's confidence soaring and his body flying, and it is up to you to keep him feeling smart as you complicate his job further. He should work the poles quickly and full of power now.

Want to isolate weave entry work? Use a target stick again, this time with no ex-pen to assist you. The dog must touch the stick by putting the first pole on his left. Click and treat along the path, then give another weave command and continue through the rest of the poles. Of course, click/treat the correct exit.

Want more speed? You might increase your dog's speed further by assigning a standard regulation entry into the poles but widening the 12-pole set in the middle only (this is the beauty of two sets of six poles). This has a lovely effect of speeding up the moderate dog, especially if you click and interrupt the set as he speeds up in the middle. You can step in with the treat as you did earlier, in agreement with his path so as to be able to continue the poles with another weave command.

As you work with a regulation configuration of 12 poles, you still have options about whether and where to widen the channel slightly. For example, you might widen the channel slightly at entry in order to work a more challenging approach angle, to help the dog when he comes out of a blind spot at speed into the poles or when he is working downhill into the weaves. You could also leave the channel closed and put up an ex-pen temporarily to build the correct habit at speed.

WEAVE POLES (CHANNEL METHOD) SUMMARY

STEP 1: One set of six channel-style poles, with channel at least 1 foot wide and ex-pens on both sides. Helper holds dog and employs eager restraint as you call dog through. Work beside dog up and back, clicking and treating correct exit. Narrow channel to 6 inches and repeat.

STEP 2: One set of six channel-style poles, with channel 6 inches wide and ex-pen on one

Twelve years old and still going strong, Spring shows the correct exit.

side only. Click as dog weaves away and treat as dog weaves back toward you. Dog's initiative takes over. Not command based! Use target stick to polish independent entry. Introduce marker for entry and click for exit

STEP 3: Two sets of six channel poles set 6 inches wide with ex-pen on one side. Sets are 15 feet apart. Handler marks entry, clicks exit and treats on way to second set. Send dog ahead, mark entry and click/treat/party at second exit. Decrease to 10 feet between sets; click/treat between. Decrease to 5 feet between sets; continue from first set to second without click/treat. Put sets together (12 poles). Work both sides of ex-pens with dog on left and dog on right.

STEP 4: Vary channel width. Add front and rear crosses between two sets. Gradually narrow

channels to in-line closed channels through 12 poles.

STEP 5: Gradually remove ex-pens by moving them away from poles, a few inches at a time, until dog no longer uses them as visual cue. Use target stick to reinforce independent correct entry. Continue varying all variables.

ABOVE: A successful day on the agility course means having fun and enjoying the time with each other. FACING PAGE: Speed, flexibility and confidence come together as this Collie maneuvers through the weave poles.

Index